SRI NITYANANDA WITH SRI GOURANGA-GADADHAR

SRI NITYANANDA
With
Sri Gouranga-Gadadhar

RADHAKRISHNA GOSWAMI

KALPAZ

Sri Nityanada with Sri Gouranga-Gadadhar

ISBN: 978-81-7835-839-0

Rs. 590

Published in 2010 in India by
Kalpaz Publications
C-30, Satyawati Nagar,
Delhi-110052
E-mail: kalpaz@hotmail.com
Phone : 9212729499

Laser Type Setting by: Rudra Computer Graphics, Delhi
Printed at : Chawla Offset Printers, Delhi

To

My son-in-law

SRI PRABIR GANGULI

and

My Sons

SRI HINDOL GOSWAMI

and

SRI ANINDYA GOSWAMI

May God be with them all the time......

Contents

Vandana

बंदे गुरुनीशभक्तानीशमीशबतारकान ।
तत् प्रकाशंश्च तत्शक्तिः कृष्णचैतन्य संगकम्।।

(In Sanskrit)

Bande Gurunish bhaktanish avatarkaan

Tat prakashangashcha Tatchchhaktih Krishnachaitanyasangakam

At first I bow to the Preceptors (of Diksha and Siksha), the Devotees of God (Sribaas and Others), the Incarnation of God (Sri Adwaitacharya and Others), Propagators of God (Sri Nityananda and Others), Strength of God (Sri Gadadhar and Others) and God-Lord Sri Krishna named Sri Krishna Chaitanyadev. (1)

Divyadvrindaranya Kalpadrumaadhah Srimadratnagara Simhasanasthou.

Srimad Radha Srila Govinda Devou presthalivih sebyamaanyou smarami.

Those who are seated on gem-pearls decorated throne under the tree Kalpa Briksha in the beautiful Divine forest of Vrindas (Vrindavan) and are lovely surrounded and served by Brajagopis, I remember from the core of the heart Srimati Radha and Srila Govinda. (2)

Sri Radhaayah pranoyamahima kidrisho banaoiba aaswyado yenadbhuta madhurima kidrisho baa madiya?

Soukhyang chaasya madanubhabatah kidrishangbeti lovattadabhabadyha samajoni Sachigarvasindhou Harindu.

'What the glory of Love of Srmati Radhika is, what She tastes with Love, what the variety and plenty of my Love is, I with mine feelings what Srimati feels, what the charm therein is, I being greedy to know those' with these three thinkings, the moonlike beautiful Sri Krishna has been appeared in the Omb-ocean of Sachimaa. (3)

"Radhakrishna pranaya vikritirhladini shaktirshma-

Dekatmanavapi-bhubi pura dehabhedang gataou tou.

Chaitanyakhyang prakatamadhuna tadwayang chaikyamaptang

Radhabhavdyuti subalitang noumi Krishnaswarupam.

Srimati Radhika is the symbol of passion and fashion power in the eternal Lila. So, Radhakrishna being one and single the Supreme Soul have admitted the difference of two entity in this earthly atmosphere. Recently, they both have become one and appeared on this earth. (4)

Jai Jai Sri Krishnachaitanya kripasindhu.

Jai Jai Nityananda agragatir bandhu.

Jaiadwaita chandrer jeevan dhanaprana.

Jai Sri Nibaas Gadadharer nidhan.

I like to shout repeatedly the sound of victory of Sri Krishnachaitanya Mahaprabhu who is kind to us like a sea, I like to repeat victorious sounds for Nityanandaprabhu who is considered a friend of advancememnts, I like to repeat the same for Sri Adwaitacharya whose life and wealth is Srichaitanyadev and I like to repeat victorious sound for Sribaas and Sri Gadadhar to whom Sri Chaitanyadev is a store house of treasure. (5)

Introduction

The life sketches of Nityananda Prabhu, Sri Gadadhar Pundit, Adwaitacharya, Sribaas, Yaban Haridas and other associates who took part in the Harinaam Movement a half millennium ago cannot be discussed without the mentions of Sri Chaitanyadev. Sri Chaitanyadev remains in the centre as the most illuminous main Character of all the associates. Therefore, Sri Nityananda Prabhu and Sri Gadadhar Pundit's lives reqire to be discussed in the light of Sri Chaitanyadev and also His other closed associates.

Vaishnavism

Let us at first discuss in brief about what various Scriptures tell about Vaishnavism (as also narrated in the Author's earlier Book Sri Chaitanyadev and Sri Gadadhar). From the dawn of this Earth, we find Brahma as a Vaishnava. According to Vaishnava beliefs, even Shiva Mahadeva was also a Parama Vaishnava.

From the collections from excavations at different places in undivided India, the deities, utensils, weapons, etc. as used by the people of ancient ages we can know or guess our past. Importantly among other things, many deities of Lord Sri Vishnu were also discovered.

The very word 'Vaishnava' is available in the great Mahabharata. It has also evidence that many of the eighteen Puaranas were composed before writing of the Mahabharata as those are referred to in the great epic.

Vaishnav means the worshipper of Lord Vishnu. In Panini's Astadhyai written in 700 B.C., we can find the word Vasudevak that expresses worshipper of Lord Vishnu. This Vasudevak and the religion of Bhagwata probably existed long before 7th century B.C. The rulers of the Gupta dynasty preferred to introduce themselves as Param Bhagawata.

In the Holy Rig Veda with the words, we find 'Idang Vishnurvichakrame' the sages prayed to Vishnu 'Vishno Sumating Bhajammahe'.

In the Yajurveda this Vishnu is described the Yagnapurusha.

In the Oiteraya Brahman Vishnu has been described the Supreme-'Vishnurparama' and 'Devanam Dwaparah' i.e. all gods and goddesses are worshipped at His door.

Even in the Srimad Bhagwatgita, known as the Gita, Lord Sri Krishna advised Arjuna-

"Ahang Hi Sarbayagnang Bhokta cha Prabhureb cha,

Na Tu Mamabhijananti Tattwenatashchyabanti Te." (9/24)

- I am the ultimate receiver and the Lord of all the things those offered to any gods but no one can apprehend the reality of mine.

- In the Gita (9/32) Lord Sri Krishna assured Partha (Arjuna) that anybody born anywhere, in any caste irrespective of in any religions who worships Me-the Ultimate, gets supreme celestial position.

Vasudeva-Vishnu-Narayana is the same and the One as per the Gita.

In the Taittariya Aranyaka - "Narayana Bidmahe, Basudevaya Dhimahi, Tanno Vishnuh Prachodayat"- I know Narayana, I meditate Him as Vasudeva, He is Vishnu, He is the Almighty and directs everything in the Universe.

Lord Sri Krishna in the Gita said to Arjuna also -

'Brishninam Vasudevohashmi'.

In the explanation by Patanjal we find - 'Asadhurmatule Krishnah ebang Jaghan Kansam Kil Vasudevah'. (6)

Goudiya Vaishnavism

Lord Gourangadev of Nabadwip became overwhelmed with the Love for Lord Sri Krishna. Sri Gourangadev established the Goudiya Vaishnavism through His associates, followers and scriptures composed by many associates, followers in Vrindavan, Srikshetra (Neelachal), Nabadwip and some other places.

He gave direct teachings to Sanatan Goswami and Roop Goswami and many others who closely got the contacts.

The thoughts were on social lives and religious simplicity so that the mere illiterate people almost living below the poverty line and socially deprived of human prestige may breathe on this earth easily like other people living on the high altitude with intellect, money and prestigious position. And the people living on higher altitude also can find easy entrance into Vaishnavism. Once Sri Chaitanyadev said wherever you are born that matters little but you must remain honest to yourself and pronounce the name of Lord Sri Krishna. Whoever once utters the name of Lord Sri Krishna he is welcomed. But, a person having born in the high families if involves in dishonest activities or does not utter the name of Lord Sri Krishna in his lips is cursed. Mahaprabhu Sri Chaitanyadev tried to remind all to think themselves as man, as human being with values because God makes all creatures in the Universe and He remains in all creations. Therefore, Vaishnavism welcomes everyone of this earth to live in peace and harmony by leaving aside all the differences still we find here and there in the world.

The most popular commander in chief in Chaitanyadev's Krishnanaam Movement was Sri Nityananda Prabhu.

1

Sri Gour Katha

The Background

The condition of society was so deplorable that it needed a change but there was none to save it. There before more than 500 years back the geopolitical stereotype of Bengal was different than it is of today. The social scenario was severe, if it is in financial sector, in agriculture, in basic education or in healthcare sector Bengal lagged behind, in addition to that it suffered draught, floods and famines too. Not only that epidemics, communal riots and invasions were other problems that cornered to the extreme darkness.

Sad but it is true that, like in other places of India, in Bengal also Brahmin and upper class people enjoyed right to oppress the other class people. People who used to run this Society behaved like local monarchs, if they thought any person crossed the regulations generated by upper class people they used to jump in to impose social sanctions. People sometime had to forget that they are human beings. On the other hand, the rulers with Islamic belief used to oppress the non – Islamic subject with their followers even at remote villages. There were also luring offers those expedited the large conversions. Suffocated Bengal was dying for want of fresh air.

Sri Adwaitacharya

Before the divine birth of Sri Gouranga Mahaprabhu, middleaged pious Kamalaksha Bhattacharya widely known as Sri Adwyaitacharya (1434-1558) observed prolonged disorder in the society. He was expecting that Lord Sri Krishna should reappear on this earth to protect the lives of the innocents and to drive out the mischief from the society as He assured in the Srimadbhagwatgita (the Gita). He worshipped Lord Sri Krishna with His favourite Tulsi leaves along with water of the holy river Ganga and prayed to Him to reappear in the world in order to establish peace. Older Adwaitacharya was eagerly waiting for reappearance of God, 'Krishnastubhagawanswam' Sri Krishna who always saves and will save the Creations from all kinds of unwanted odds in the Universe.

People in Nabadwip

A handful people only used to worship Lord Sri Krishna in Nabadwip and also in whole Bengal. Worshipping of the goddesses of Power and Strength and Lord Shiva Mahadeva was in practice. However, most of the worshippers of Shakti and common men used to consume huge amount of liquor, meat etc. and indulged many other types of ill habits in the name of worshiping the goddess in many names. People forgot their culture. Most of them were satisfied with the then present lifestyle. Hardly one thought for the future development, art, education and literature. None considered to get prepared oneself to protect from the hands of tyranny and oppression from the then society and political adverse situations. Rather, their ill motivated habits would tend to effect on the innocent, pious and peace loving people. People had also to forget any other kind of amusement. Sometime people hardly dared to think that they are also human beings and they have the right to live peacefully in own land.

Adwaitacharya used to worship Lord Sri Krishna with Tulsi leaf and holy water of the Ganga by praying to God to keep His words as He assured in the Gita (Chap. IV Sl. 7 & 8)-

Yada Yada hi dharmasya glanirbhabati Bharata.

Abhyuthana adharmasya tadatmaanaang srijamyaham.

Paritranaya saadhunang bianashaya cha duskritaam.

Dharma sansthapanaaya sambhabaami yuge yugey.

Having experiences and observing lot of irregularities in the then society more than 500 years back Adwaitacharya had nothing to do except worshipping the Great Paritrata, the Saviour, Lord sri Krishna as He assured in the Gita that He would reappear in the most unwanted deplorable situation of the Society. Adwaitacharya so, worshipped Lord Sri Krishna and was in search of a personality who could save Bengal and rest of the other places from all types of irregularities in the Society.

The Divine Birth

Sri Chaitanyadev was incarnated on the earth on the evening of Dol Purnima (Holi Festival) of Falguna in 1407 Saka (1486 A.D., Bengali Years 892) at Nabadwip in the district of Nadia, Bengal in the lap of Sachimaa. Although few of Nabadwip did care little for uttering the name of Lord Sri Krishna, people on the very day for Holi were engaged in Harinaam Kirtan as usual practice as also there was Lunar eclipse in the evening. (7)

His name was Vishwambhar in tune of elder's name Vishwarup. For fair complexion Vishwambhar was called Gouranga or Gour in short. Sri Gourangadev's nickname was Nemai from childhood. Nemai indicates a name from the Neem tree, a bitter thing, so that even Jomraj cannot have any interest to the child because after Vishwarup's Sannyas this child remained as only living child. His parents Jagannath Mishra and Sachidevi, daughter of renowned astrologer Nilambar Chakraborty, had eight daughters and two sons. The daughters did not survive but sons Vishwarup and Vishwambhar survived. Among all the issues, Vishwambhar was the youngest. However, later Sri Gourangadev also took Sannyas. At Sannyas, Keshav Bharati, the preceptor awarded the name **Sri Krishna Chaitanya** to Nemai Pundit. People and the devotees used to call Him in short as **Sri Chaitanyadev**.

Vishwarup the Elder Brother

Vishwarup, seven to eight years' elder to Sri Gouranga, being learned in old scriptures like the Upanishads and the Srimad Bhagawat Geeta (the Gita) and the Others at his sixteen left the home and became an ascetic. Reasearchers say that he was named as

Shankaranya and went to Southwestern part of of the Country.

Nemai before lunchtime used to bring or call the elder brother Vishwarup from the house of Adwaitacharya in Nabadwip where Vishwarup before leaving home for Sannyas engaged himself in discussing and exchanging opinions on topics on the Upanishads, the Srimadbhagwatgita and other Scriptures with deep knowledge.

Thus, in turn, Adwaitacharya got the opportunity of glimpses of the future possible Leader. Because this 52 years' older than Nemai was in search of a Rescuer who would come this world to save the mankind from all ill habits and ill practices prevailed.

Nemai's Childhood

Gouranga had shown varieties of Lila at the childhood. He with Gadadhar, Mukunda, Sanjay and others of the locality played on the grounds, near the ghat of the river Ganga, sometimes took part in swimming with all the friends. He forced to take whatever materials were ready for offering to the gods and goddesses at the ghat by the little girls devotees.

Beginning of Nemai's Education

Nemai's education started in the hand of Purandar Pundit but after elder son Vishwarup's leaving home the parents once did not prefer to allow their only remaining son Nemai to learn much. Understanding parents' desire to keep him tied in family atmosphere as an ordinary son without any scope of high and deep education Nemai chose a dustbin to sit in protest by saying

– I am not getting proper education, so how I shall know what to do or what not to do. At last, the parents assured and started to send Nemai to the Tole of Gangadas Pundit.

Father's Demise

Nemai's childhood could not continue for a long time as father Jagannath Mishra after, Nemai's ceremony of wearing the sacred thread breathed his last by assuring the only child crying for for helplessness that Sri Ram Chandra would look after. Nemai then returning to normal life started to continue education and teachings to others.

Raghunath Siromani

Mahaprabhu have written many things. We know the episode that during His studentship dropped own writings on Nayashastra (Logic) into the water of the Ganga. One day he was travelling on boat with Raghunath Siromani another batchmate. Raghunath, a proficient scholar in Nayashastra told Gouranga that he wrote a book of analytical appreciation of Didhiti's Nayashastra. Nemai had also written an analytical note on the same subject. Raghunath wanted to listen what Gouranga had written. Gouranga, unforuntely carried the script and without any hesitation started to read the script sitting on the side of the boat. Having listened to it, Raghunath discovered that Gouranga's explanationary note was far better than that of his own and started to weep. Gourangadev enquired the reason behind his weeping. He replied that if Gouranga's Script comes out no one would read his write up as the quality of Gouranga's writing is far better than his and would be acceptable by the readers. Therefore, his efforts would be of no use. Seeing Raghunath Siromoni crying for fame Nemai consoled him not to cry for earthly fame but for God. Nemai then without any delay tore own manuscript into pieces and threw it like a stone into the water of the Ganga. Such a noble Mahaprabhu was in His studentlife.

At the age of sixteen Nemai in Nabadwip became a renowned teacher in Sanskrit.

Vidyavilas

A time when Nemai used catch friends on streets, in the *hut* (periodical market place) and at the *ghats* of the Ganga and ask difficult questions from old scriptures. He did not spare own prtner Gadadhar and Mukunda also.

Prabhu boley Gadadhar aaji jaaha ghar

Kali bujhibaang tumi aasiha satwar. -Yes Gadadhar, today I have seen your capacity. Come tomorrow after reading and knowing all these. (8)

He used to judge the limited number of people who were in practice to worship Lord Sri Krishna only. Even older Sri Krishna devotee Sribaas was not spared from the questionings of Nemai Pundit. This was the period of Vidyavilas. Yet, Mahaprabhu Nemai knew who were the real devotees like Sribaas in Nabadwip and offered due respect to them also.

Antarjaami Prabnu chitta jaanen sobaar.

Sribaasadi dekhilei karey Namaskar. – Mahaprabhu was aware of everybody's mind but He offered due respect to older devotee Sribaas also. (9)

Lakshmipriya Devi

Some days later, His marriage took place with Lakshmipriya Devi daughter of Ballav Acharya a pious and scholar personality of Nabadwip. This, perhaps, was according to Nemai's own preference and arrangement by Mother Sachidevi.

Pundit Keshab Kashmiri

Once, one self-styled digvijoyee Keshab Kashmiri came in Nabadwip and among the probable contesters' list collected by his men, he noticed at the top the name of 16/17 years' old Nemai Pundit there. One fine afternoon, while wandering in Nabadwip town and different *ghats* on the bank on the holy Ganga he found Nemai Pundit engaged in discussing various topics with some students and fellow scholars. He found Nemai a mere boy of teenage teaching all with His melodious voice and scholarly expertness. Keshab's companion informed him that it is he whose name topped the list of scholars of Nabadwip.

Kashmiriji introduced himself as Digvijoyee (world conqueror) and Nemai Pundit showed due respect to him and asked him to describe the glory of the Ganga.

Keshab Kashmiri then, by composing a poem on the holy Ganga started to recite with emotion. The poem contained one hundred slokas with which he prayed the holy Ganga.

Mahattang Gangayah Satatamidmaabhaati Nitaraang

Yadesha Sri Vishnoscharana Kamalotpatti Subhaga.

Dwitwiya Sri Lakshmiriba

suranarairchyacharana

Bhabanibharturya Siroshi Bibhatyadbhutaguna.
(10)

Nemai found five faults of grammar and rhetoric in the poem. As for example, in the word, 'Bhabanibharturya' Bhabani itself is the wife of Bhaba (Lord Shiva) and then husband of Bhabani appears to be another husband of Bhabani that becomes meaningless.

At last, the conqueror scholar Keshab Kashmiri being defeated to a boy of yesterday, like Nemi Pundit could not make out how it was possible for Nemai to recollect a few specific lines once listening from one hundred slokas he recited and detected five faults. He was rather shocked.

Humbly Nemai Pundit consoled him and advised to give up vanity forever and to take shelter of Lord Sri Krishna.

Visit in East Bengal

Afterwards Nemai went to East Bengal (now Bangladesh) to offer education and to arrange future programme. Nemai travelled Dacca, Faridpur on the bank of the river Padma and Srihatta the district from where father Jagannath Mishra and other scholars immigrated to Nabadwip.

He travelled in Vikrampore, Subarna village, Egarsindur, Betal etc. and established schools for offering education. Students from different corners of the Country started to assemble at the education centers in order to have direct learnings from the eminent Nemai Pundit.

There at Srihatta Tapan Mishra met and requested Nemai Pundit to stay in East Bengal for some more days and not to leave them. Gourangadev advised him to settle later in Varanasi and there, Nemai would meet him again. However, in the mean time, Lakshmipriyadevi expired suddenly by a snakebite in Nabadwip.

Nemai Returned to Nabadwip

Nemai returned home but could not find Laxmilike wife Lakshmipriya there and understood that she has left this earth. Perhaps Nemai could sense this accident and so returned from East Bengal hurriedly. Nemai then engaged Himself in more learning, teaching and discussions throughout the whole days with other scholars in Nabadwip. Students from different corners of the country assembled in Nabadwip to receive teachings from famous Nemai Pundit. They learned not only to learn properly but they learned to maintain their own rites for own religion and complete faith in God and complete surrender to Lord Sri Krishna.

Vishnupriya Devi

Sachidevi again arranged the marriage for Sri Gouranga with another beautiful girl Vishnupriya Devi, daughter of Sri Sanatan Mishra a well renowned Pundit who was known as Rajpundit.

Buddhimanta Khan, a Zeminder (some say, earlier known as Subuddhi Roy) fond of Sri Gourangadev, took the entire responsibility of all the expenditure of the marriage. The marriage became a memorable event in Nabadwip like a marriage of a prince.

Buddhimanta Khan later became a pious devotee as an orinary mendicant ascetic and settled in Vrindavan. He worked hard to discover the old abandoned Temples and Deities from the bushes of the forests in Vrindavan with direction from Sri Gouranga Mahaprabhu.

Nemai as a Teacher

In Nabadwip Gourangadev continued teachings at the centre near Sanjay-Mukunda's house at their Chandi Mandap and got immense fame for the scholarly teaching capacity. Students from various corners of the Country used to come to Nabadwip.

Nemai at Gaya

Taking permission from Sachidevi almost two years after the marriage Nemai Pundit, with some followers and maternal uncle Chandra Sekhar, went to Gaya for giving ***Pinda*** to the deceased father and ancestors.

Ishwarpuri at Gaya

Gourangadev visited the sign of holy ***Padapadma*** of Shri Vishnu and thinking that once this foot of Lord Sri Krishna bestowed on Boli and Mahaprabhu became almost mad in love for Lord. After performing the holy rituals towards the ancestors Nemai found there, by chance, Ishwarpuri.

Earlier Gourangadev once met him on way to the Ganga in Nabadwip. He participated in discussions on Lord Sri Krishna while Ishwarpuri read out his own writing Krishnalilamrita to Gadadhar Pundit and some others at Gopinath Acharya's house during his stay there for a few days.

The Initiation

Gourangadev at Gaya observing Ishwarpuri's profound devotion in Lord Sri Krishna became overwhelmed and wanted to get initiation and thus Ishwarpuri by giving the Sri Krishna Mantra to Sri Gouranga became the preceptor of Sri Gourangadev. He got the mantra of Lord Sri Krishna. After visiting *Pret Gaya, Yudhisthir Gaya, Uttar Manas, Bheem Gaya, Shiva Gaya, Brahma Gaya, Sorasha Gaya* etc. and offering respects Sri Gourangadev started for Nabadwip. On the way He visited the birth place of Ishwarpuri at Kumarhatta near todays' Kanchrapara in West Bengal. Sri Gourangadev took clays from the pond where the Preceptor once lived. Then Sri Gourangadev returned in Nabadwip but as a changed person who always think of God Lord Sri Krishna.

Nemai Appeared to be a new Personality in Nabadwip

From then Gourangadev appeared to be a new personality and can visualise God everywhere all the time and started to chant, dance, cry for Lord Sri Krishna.

One fine morning some devotees of Sri Krishna at a flower garden were plucking flowers and Tulsi leaves for worshipping Sri Krisha. There were present Gadadhar, Gopinath, Ramai, Sribaas and some others. Sriman Pundit hurriedly came to them. He told them as an announcement, that their Sri Gouranga has been changed to a new personality and has become modest one. He does not show any audacity and tease anybody by asking any question. He becomes mad whenever listens the name of Lord Sri Krishna. He also added that, in the afternoon at

Shuklambar's residence Sri Gouranga should express the experiences of Gaya tour and any body can attend the meeting. Sri Gouranga did not mention anybody's name in particular. So, Gadadhar planed to listen Mahaprabhu's reporting from behind.

Nemai at Shuklambar's Residence

In the afternoon Gadadhar took shelter by hiding himself at Shuklambar Brahmachari's residence for hearing what Sri Gouranga says. Sri Gouranga came to the house with tilting body, as the heart is always full with the thoughts of Lord Sri Krishna. He cries often – "Where is Sri Krishna. Krishna was seen here, now where He has gone!" Other some followers feeling Lord Sri Krishna's presence everywhere but not easily visible were also weeping in love for God. Gourangadev advised Murari and Sadashiva who were in practice of worshipping Lord Sri Krishna from very childhood like Gadadhar Pundit - "Murari, Sadashiva please continue to worship God with more respect". Mahaprabhu again started to cry for Lord Sri Krishna and fainted at times.

Lifelong Companion Gadadhar Pundit

Gadadhar Pundit, however, could not restrain his ecstasy. With his head bowed down, he continued to cry very loudly. Hearing his pitiful sobbing, Sri Gouranga enquired- 'Who is there weeping?'

Murari answered-'It is Gadadhar. Yours Gadadhar.'

With the words 'yours Gadadhar' one can easily understand how Gadadhar Pundit was closet to Sri Gourangadev.

Sri Gourangadev called Gadadhar with much affection and Gadadhar leaving the hiding corner of the room of Suklambar Brahmachari came out and fell on the feet of Gourangadev. He told Gadadhar –

'Your life is successful as you have been worshipping Lord Sri Krishna from the childhood. Alas, I have wasted the time without worshipping Sri Krishna.' (11)

By saying this, Mahaprabhu Sri Gouranga embraced Gadadhar in great love and again fainted.

Sri Gouranga Mahaprabhu, upon coming from Gaya Dham, day and night floated in the ocean of love for Sri Krishna. Gadadhar, upon seeing the Gourangadev showering of tears in love for Sri Krishna, also began to cry in love.

One day Sri Gadadhar Pundit brought some pan (betal leaf) to Sri Gauranga, who, in an exuberance of love for Sri Krishna asked him- "Gadadhar! Where is that beautiful blackish Boy Who is dressed in yellow garments?" After asking this, Sri Gouranga began to shed tears, looked here and there but could not find.

Gadadhar respectfully suggested- "He is in your heart."

Hearing this, Sri Gouranga began to tear his chest with his nails, but Gadadhar Pundit quickly grabbed his hands. Mahprabhu said to him, "Gadadhar! Leave me. I cannot remain a moment more not seeing Sri Krishna."

Gadadhar replied, "Just try to be a little patient and please calm Yourself. Sri Krishna would come any moment here and everywhere."(12)

On the new moon day of Baisakh in 1408 Saka (in 1487 A.D.) Sri Gadadhar Pundit was born Gadadhar was one of the pioneers who used to worship Lord Sri Krishna and believed in His Divine Love. Some of devotees, till, worship Gadadhar as Radharani the main strength of Lord Sri Krishna as well as main strength of Sri Gourangadev. Sri Gadadhar was the constant companion of Mahaprabhu from the time of their childhood.

His parents were Madhab Mishra and Ratnadevi. Madhab Mishra came to Nabadwip from Chattragram (Chittagong) of East Bengal and settled at the holy place with scopes of learning and offering education. They were very pious couple, and they were disciples of Madhabendrapuri, the then the most renowned preacher and pioneer of the name of Lord Sri Krishna's Divine Love.

Gadadhar-Gouranga lived in closer houses in the same locality. Gadadhar's mother Ratnavati Devi often used to meet Sachidevi. Sachidevi took her as own sister. Gouranga and Gadadhar used to play together on the yard nearer to where their mothers generally used to sit and talk each other sometimes at Mahaprabhu's house and sometimes at Gadadhara's house. They both studied together at the same school. Nemai could not remain without Gadadhar even for a moment and Gadadhar likewise could not stand the separation for a single moment from Nemai. Naturally, younger Gadadhar Pundit got much affection from Nemai Pundit. Both of them had due respect for each other.

Sachimaa knew all these and then seeing Pundit Gadadhar's ability to control her only remainig son Nemai became very pleased with him. She thought herself -

"Gadadhar is just a boy but he is very intelligent and capable of handling Nemai. I am frightened to go before Nemai in these moods. But Gadadhar has very cleverly pacified him."

Sachimaa told Gadadhar Pundit - "Gadadhar! You must please remain with Nemai always. If you stay with Him then I won't have to worry."

"Bara tusta hoila aai Gadadhar prati.

E mata subuddhi sisu naahi dekhi kati".

And

Aai boley baap tumi sarbada thaakiba

Chhariya uhaar sanga kothao na jaaibaa. – Sachimaa became very pleased to Gadadhar a rare modest boy. Again she requested him to remain with Nemai all the time, not to leave Nemai for a single moment. (13)

Since then Gadadhar never left the company of Sri Gouranga and even after Nemai's Sannyas Gadadhar Pundit remained at Puri in order to serve his beloved Nemai and he kept the words of a mother uptill their last moments on this earth.

Gangadas Pundit

Sri Gouranga's love for Sri Krishna, day after day, increased. He forgot to go to Tole (education centre) to teach the students. He could not pay proper attention to the family and hard reality of social life. The elderly teacher Gangadas Pundit, once a friend of father Jagannath Mishra came and suggested Nemai to restart the Tole as the students intending to have proper coaching from Sri Gouranga came from different corners of the Country. He also raised a pertinent question, how the expenditure of the members of the big family consisting of mother, wife and also students, guests and devotees coming almost regularly from distant places can be managed? With due respect young Nemai admitted it and restarted the Tole for offering coachings.

Nemai's Method of Teachings and Ratnagarva Pundit

The techniques of offering teachings were marvelous one. He took the students at *Chandi Mandap*, at porticos of other residents, on walking on streets, at the *ghats* of the Ganga, at open space under the vast blue sky or under a tree with green leaves, flowers and fruits of different colors in different seasons.

One day with the students while in discussion in the unique method in Nabadwip Nemai Pundit with students and own people halted at the yard of the house of Ratnagarva Pundit and continued discussion on lessons. After sometime, the owner of the house Ratnagarva returned home by reciting a few lines of the Srimad Bhagawata in his own

"Shyamang hiranyaparidhing
banamalyabahrdhatu prabal
nataveshamnubratangse,

Binyastahastamitayena yunanabjam
karnotpalala kapolmukhabjalasan." (14)

On hearing the melodious and poetic recitation, Nemai fainted in love for Lord Sri Krishna. It is obvious that Gadadhar remains where Gouranga remains or moves. Seeing fainted Nemai, Gadadhar somehow nursed with the help of the students and requested Ratnagarva to stop. However, Sri Gouranga getting sense again requested Ratnagarva to recite the very lines.

Poetic recitation of the Sloka by Ratnagarva Pundit

The very lines were of a picture on the incidence of Sri Krishna darshan by the wives of Yagnik (burnt offering) Brahmins. Their villages were nearer to gazing grounds where young Sri Krishna with elder brother Sri Balaram and other Gopa children from the houses of milkmen use to allow the cows and calves for gazing. Coming to the grounds perhaps they have eaten up the tiffin supplied by their mothers. In the noon, they again felt hungry and young Sri Krishna guessed, sure the Brahmin ladies in the nearer villge have prepared food for their husbands, children and other members of their families. With Krishna's advice, team of hungry children at first went to them but the ladies rejected their requests of surrendering any food. On this refusal, Krishna advised them - Do struggle until you achieve the prayed things. Go and ask for. Go repeatedly, once you would succeed'. He also advised them to inform the ladies of the Brahmins that son Gopal of Nandagopa, God Himself has favoured them by asking for food. He needs the food. Realizing the eternal truth the women came to Nandatanaya Sri Krishna with the entire food they cooked for their husbands and children. They, coming over the gazing field saw all the Gopa children, Sri Krishna and Sri Balaram on the bank of the Yamuna River.

The description in the recitation of Ratnagarva was : His complexion is beautiful dark blue. He is wearing a yellow coloured dress. There is garland with the flowers plucked from nearby forests around His neck. He is decorated as an actor of a certain drama with peacock's feather, metals like gold, corals and others. He has placed one of his hands on shoulder of another Gopa and circling another hand with the lotus of the eternal creativity. Earrings under the ears, hair clinging from the head are disarranged and the eternal laughter remaining on the lips of Sri Krishna".(14)

Nemai fainted again

Nemai fainted and again coming to senses requested Ratnagarva to recite the sloka. Ratnagarva did the same and again Nemai fainted. This process continued for some time and Nemai became almost mad. Gadadhar seeing Nemai's condition beyond control, said to Ratnagarva to stop the recitation-

Na pariah aar balilen Gadadhar

Savey beri basilen Vishwambhar. - Gadadhar advised - Do not recite any longer. All present sat encircling Nemai (15).

Gadadhar somehow managed to take Gouranga at home where anxious mother Sachidevi is waiting for her son eagerly.

Again Nemai's Teaching to Students

This situation occurred often. It became a regular incidence. Nemai sometime cried – Where is Lord Sri Krishna? - Where He is? - Where I could get Him? – Nemai always was in search of Him and became fainted many a time for love of Lord Sri Krishna. Nemai was so profoundly occupied with the feelings of God Sri Krishna that students cannot get annlytical lessons as instead Nemai teaches them-

Bolo Krishna bhojo Krishna suno Krishna naam.
Aharnishi SriKrishna charan karo dhyan. – Say Krishna, worship Krishna and hear the name of Krishna. Day and night meditate the feet of Sri Krishna. (16)

Gadadhar Pundit always remains with Nemai

Gadadhar Pundit always remains at the side of Nemai so that Nemai does not get any hurt while He becomes occupied with the feelings of Sri Krishna's existence surrounding Him. He cannot have any sense or faints and falls on the floors of streets or yards or on the ghats of the Ganga. Gadahar Pundit remains always to guard and holds his life long friend unhurt.

Nemai appeared to be a new personality who can see God everywhere and started to sing, dance, cry for Lord Sri Krishna. He did not remain as Nemai Pundit, neither as Vishwambhar, nor Gouranga only but became Mahaprabhu Sri Gouranga who was mad for Lord Sri Krishna. On the other side the people, few in number, who once wished that Nemai Pundit should have faith in Sri Krishna instead of practices of teasing, embarrassing the Krishna loving people in times were surprised to note the rapid changes, the modesty and the attraction to Sri Krishna, love for sri Krishna, thirst for the 'entwined in bliss Krishna and Radha'.

Harinaam Movement

Then Nemai started the Harinaam Movement from own house then at Suklambar Brahmachari's house and at last at the house of Sribaas in Nabadwip. With this movement people in hundreds flocked together and the whole day and night along with all the followers encircling Sri Gouranga Mahaprabhu, they chanted Sri Krishna's name and glory. Singing and dancing for Lord Sri Krishna Gouranga Mahaprabhu becomes overwhelmed and Gadadhar and other devotees would hold Him so that He does not fall on the floors and get any hurt on the Divine Body.

The most beloved Haridas

The most beloved Haridas, known as Yaban Haridas joined the team. Earlier Haridas was brought up by a pious Muslim family at Buran Village. It is learnt that from his childhood Haridas joined Sri Adwaitacharya. Haridas was born in 1371 Saka in a village Buran in the district Nadia. His father Sumati Thakur breathed his last when he was only a six years' old. Then his mother Gouridevi had also courted death by burning herself on her husband's funeral pyre. Haridas at his six became parentless and a pious Muslim family brought him up as their own son. Having shelter like a son in a Muslim family he got the scope to have knowledge in Islamic belief.

Afterwards being aware of God's Oneness and Glory he met Sri Adwaitacharya at Shantipur and requested him to give him Krishna Mantra. After repeated requests and having observed some signs of Bhakti, Adwaitacharya gave him the Mantra-

Hare Krishna Hare Krishna Krishna Krishna Hare Hare
Hare Rama Hare Rama Rama Rama Hare Hare

With this Mantra, modest Haridas settled in a hut in the village Kulia and started to take the mantra on rosary almost all the time. He was familiar to others as

Yaban Haridas. Once, a local Kazi ordered him not to utter 'Hare Krishna'. He denied to do so and then Kazi ordered his men to beat with sticks in Baish Bazar. However, Haridas did not leave the name of Lord Sri Krishna from his lips and somehow survived with uttering 'Hare Krishna' mantra.

The house of Sribaas

With Gadadhar Sri Gouranga Mahaprabhu met Adwaitacharya in the meantime because he earnestly prayed to God for His reappearance as a rescuer of the mankind from all types of irregularities in the society. Adwaitacharya greeted Mahaprabhu and Mahaprabhu greeted him in presence of Gadadhar Pundt and Mukunda. Adwaitacharya went to his residence at Shantipur in order to wait for the possibilities of the Samkirtan Movement.

The house of Sribaas now became full of grandeur with the new inclusion of Haridas. Now Sri Gourangadev engages Himself in Kirtan and dance at Sribaas angan with a large team. Still Mahaprabhu awaited Adwaitacharya, the pioneer of the movement and getting the information that the Samkirtan has already getting the maturity. The Team was comprised of older and experienced devotee Adwaitacharya, polite and devotee of Lord Sri Krishna and Nemai's lifetime companion Gadadhar Pundit, a man dedicated life only in Harinaam Haridas, Basudev Dutta and his brother having melodious voice, singer and devotee Mukunda, a devotee of Sri Ramchandraji Murai, others like Chandrasekhar, Sadashiv, Sanjay, an ordinary banana cone seller Sridhar, mendicant like Suklambar Brahmachari and many others who lived in Nabadwip and the sourrounding areas. All devotees of Lord Sri Krishna were present in the house of the senior devotee Sribaas with his brothers.

Deplorable condition of the Society

The time was running in acute deplorable condition. People were fed up with social, political, financial conditions and various differences, divisions of castes, religions, languages, ethnic roots etc. Torture on innocents by anti-socials and people of rulers' religion and rulers' representatives at times continued. Oppression by the rich on the poor and middle class people was regular phenomena. The people who lived on hard labour throughout the days used to get meagre amount of wages. They were denied respect of human being. Absence of Human rights and human respect were paralising the society. There was no signle effort of any development in need of society as a whole.

No other way left for the Unity in Society

To Sri Gourangadev had only one option open that to bring all under an umbrella of Harinaam Movement. He realized that, initially all are to unite and then all would understand to offer and get respect as human to each other. Afterwards all would get enthusiasm for participating in eatablishing the society in all spheres of life. With Harinaam Movement only people of different corners may unite themselves. This was the only medicine that left open to Him and the associates.

Was Sri Gouranga Mahaprabhu Mad?

Sri Gouranga Mahaprabhu with all associates sang kirtan and danced and cried for Lord Krishna and sometime became fainted and sometime appeared to be mad in love for Lord Sri Krishna. The neighbouring people started to gossip that Nemai is ill and so many of them by own suggested Sachimaa to tie her son with ropes or to consult with a Vaidya (physician) for her son's treatment.

Keho boley mahabaai bandhibaar torey,

Pundit tomaar chitta ki loi aamaarey. - Oneday Gouranga Mahaprabhu asked Sribaas- "Is it true that I have become abnormal! Do I need proper treatment?" (17)

Sribaas knew that such a God loving and rare scholar personality is imminent for the Movement otherwise people would not feel the actual necessity of joining with them. Sri Gouranga Mahaprabhu's love for Lord Sri Krishna without expecting anything but to grace the glory of God is also the urgent need for deeper devotion and that would for the betterment of the disorderedly society.

Haasi boley Sribaas Pundit – bhalo bhaai,

Tomaar yemata baai, aami taha chai. – Sribaas replied laughingly to Sri Gourangadev – "We need it and we all should become mad for Sri Krishna." (18)

The Samkirtan Movement Escalated to a Peak

The Samkirtan Movement escalated to a peak and waves of it reached all the pilgrim places of the country. Gouranga Mahaprabhu with the associates at Sribaas angan remain fully engaged in Samkirtan day and night. Sribaas himself offered his house for this Samkirtan.

One night Mahaprabhu got signs in a dream that somebody is coming. He dreamt that a great Abadhut with a large figure wearing a dress in blue colour stepped down at the door from a golden chariot.

On the other hand, at Vrindavan after roaming the whole India for last twenty years Nityananda felt that in Nabadwip Sri Gouranga Mahaprabhu has started Samkirtan Movement and He needs him. Then Nityananda arrived in Nabadwip.

(Regarding Gadadhar Pundit more information are available in Sri Chaitnyadev and Sri Gadadhar published by Kalpaz Publications, New Delhi)

2

Nityananda Katha

The Birth of Nityananda

Nityananda was born on Tuesday; the 12th/(13th) of January in 1474 (1395 Saka, in the month of Magha Sukla Traodashi in Bengali Sal seems to be 880) in the village of Ekchakra now Virchandrapur in the north of district Birbhum. His father a learned and honest Harai (Mukunda) Pundit of Sandilya Gotra (Bandyopadhyay-Banerjee) known as Haru Ojha and mother was Srimati Padmadevi. Both were also pious.

Parama udaar dui Brahman-brahmani,
Taar gharey Nityananda janmila aapani.- In the house of benevolent Brahmin couple Nityananda was born himself. (19)

They had seven sons. They were Nityananda, Krishnanda, Sarbananda, Brahmananda, Purnananda, Premananda and Vishuddhananda. The Eldest son Nityananda's nickname was Kuber.

Nityananda's Childhood

In the childhood, he was fond of playing with friends near a Shiva Temple at the end of village Ekchakra. He was fond of playing of acting dramas from the stories of the Ramayana and the Bhagawata etc. Puranas with all mates. One of the children from behind a tree shouts as Divine voice.

Janmibaang aami giya Mathura-Vrindavaney.- I am taking birth in Mathura-Vrindavan. (20)

One day at the time of acting as Lakshman in Indrajit Badh drama composed spontaniously by himself Nityananda fainted. It was an unnatural fainting as after reasonable time the actor did not come in normalcy. The friends called the adults from the village. All the villagers including Padmadevi and Harai Pundit rushed to their playground and tried their best by spreading water on the closed eyes of Kuber to bring his senses but failed. At last, one of the children co-actors as in the role of Hanumanji ran into a jungle and brought some bushes. One actor like a Vaidya touched some petals at the nose of Kuber and thereafter he woke up.

Henamatey sishukaal hoitey Nityananda,
Krishnalila whi aar na karey ananda. – From very childhood Nityananda gets joy from Sri Krishna's Lila only. (21)

One Mendicant Vaishnav arrrived

At the age of only twelve reached a mendicant Vaishnav in their house and for his service elder son Nityananda was given charge. The mendicant was very pleased with the hospitality of the family and with the services rendered by Nityananda. At the time of leaving the house of Harai Ojha, he begged something.

Nyasi boley eka bhiksha achaye aamar,
Nityanandapita boley ye ichchha tomaar. – The mendicant begged one thing and Nityananda's father said to him-as you wish.(22)

The old aged mendicant begged Nityananda for his company and assistance during his travelling on foot throughout the vast land. Nityananda with his devotion and service to him proved that he had the capability to be a trusted and dependable company of the mendicant. The ascetic having vast knowledge assured that there would be no difficulty for his further learning in different Scriptures. At that time, the people could not decline any pious mendicant Vaishnav's prayer for anything.

Although they had seven sons but every son is more than the hearts of any parents specially, the eldest one becomes a valuable partner of mother and father for the family. Thinking separation of Nityananda, they got much pain in hearts. However, the parents at last, with lot of aches in hearts agreed to leave their elder son Nityananda with him.

Aailaa Sannyasisthan Nityananda pita,
Nyasirey dilen putra noaiaa maathaa. At last father of Nityananda gave his son in the hands of the mendicant and bowed his head to him.(23).

Nityananda accompanied the Mendicant Vaishnav

Nityananda at his twelve left home forever with the mendicant Vaishnav. The whole Universe is waiting for such Personalities who sacrifice themselves everything and work for the betterment and benefit of the lives.

Father Harai Ojha had the shock that appeared to be more deeper than that of mother Padmadevi. Primarily the shock exposedly continued for three months to Harai Ojha because his elder son used give company to him in all kinds of work, especially during shopping, going to the houses for priestly works and keeping invitations etc.

After Bakreswar Nityananda moved alone

Nityananda with the mendicant arrived up to Bakreswar in the Birbhum district. From Bakreswar Nityananda alone (ekeswar) had to travel through Baidyanath, Gaya, and then Varanasi on foot.

Prathamey chalila Prabhu tirtha Bakreswar,
Tobey Baidyanath boney gelaa ekeswar - At first they reached Bakreswar, then Nityananda reached alone at Baidyanath Dham. (24)

It is also noteworthy that Mahaprabhu Sri Chaitanyadev around this time was born in Nabadwip. The further information about the mendicant is not available. Nityananda on his way of long tour on foot had to receive lot of obstacles, to confront with different situations and gained varied experiences during his travelling. He travelled the whole of the Country for a long twenty years. In these twenty years, sometime he had to live on fasting or only on water or milk or with whatever food received. Sometime he had to take rest or sleep under any tree in any forest or in cave or at any bank of a river or at any portico or a shelter in of any house.

Nityananda Travelled at different Places in the Country

He travelled Baidyanath, Gaya, bathing at Prayag, Baranasi, remembering Lord Sri Krishna at Mathura-Vrindavan, remembering Pandavas and Kouravas at Hastinapore, then turned towards Dwarka where Sri Krishna lived. It took a lot of time. He went to Sindhupur, Matsya Tirtha, Shivakanchi, Vishnukanchi and other places.

Shivakanchi Vishnukanchi gela Nityananda,

Dekhi haase duijaney mahamatta - Nityananda went Shivakanchi Vishnukanchi and both of them became joyful. (25)

Here we can guess that he came across the mendicant again or any other personality having strong faith in God.

Again, Nityananda came to Kurukshetra. From Provas, Bishala, Brahmatirtha, Chakratirtha, Prachi Saraswati he arrived at Noimisharanya. Then he turned to Ayodhya the place of Sri Ramchandra. He bathed in water of the river Koushiki and went to Pulaha Ashram and the forest where Sri Ramchandra walked with Sita devi, Lakshman and Guhak Chandal. He bathed in the Gomati, Gandaki and Saila tirtha, then went to Mahendra Hill and bowed his head to Bhagawan Parsuram. Then he reached Haridwar where the Bhagirathi Ganga starts to flow through the plains.

Again, from Haridwar he started his journey to Pampa, Vimarathi and thereafter Sapta Godavari, Benu tirtha. From there, he arrived at Sri Parbat where in disguise of a couple of Brahmins Hara-Parvati resided.

Nityananda with Madhabendrapuri, Ishwarpuri and Others

Once in the western India, accidentally he came across the pioneer of Vaishnav Preacher Madhabendra Puri with his disciples like Ishwarpuri and others. This Ishwarpuri was Mahaprabhu's preceptor.

Donhe murchha hailen dohaar darshaney,
Kandayey Ishwarpuri adi sishysaganey. – Both Nityananda and Madhabendrapuri finding each other cried in love and other disciples including Ishwarpuri also cried in joy for their union. (26)

Nityananda kahey yata tirtha karilaam,
Samyak taahaar phal aaji paailaam,

Nayaney dekhinu Madhabendrer charan,
E prem dekhia dhanya aamaar jeevan. - And with full devotion, Nityananda explained that it was a fortune for him that he could see Madhbendrapuri. It is a result of pilgrimages. (27)

Some say that Nityananda spent a long time with the spiritual team of devotees of Lord Sri Krishna and he got initiation from Madhabendra Puri. (Some say Nityananda received initiation from Lakshipati, the Preceptor of Madhabendrapuri, some also said that Shankarshanpuri was the Preceptor of Nityanandaprabhu.)

Madhabendraprati Nityananda Mahasaya,

Guru buddhi byatirikta aar na karaya - Nityananda as a gentleman regarded the pioneer Vaishnav Madhabendrapuri as only preceptor and nothing else. (28)

After some days of Bhajan, Kirtan and Pujan Madhbendrapuri went towards the river Sarajoo and Nityananda with the sweet memories of the days passed with the Vaishnavas and Madhabendrapuri a prominent devotee of Lord Sri Krishna went towards Rameswaram.

Nityananda to Mathura-Vrindavan

An almost a changed personality Nityananda after a bath at Dhanus Tirtha arrived at Rameswaram. From there, he visited Vijayanagar, Mayapuri Avanti and the Godavari. Then he arrived at Jeeor Nrisinghadeva, Trimalla and the Temple of Kurmanaath. Afterwards he found the flag is flying afar on the top of the Temple of Lord Jagannath in Neelachal. Having a full darshan of Jagannath, Balaram and Subhadra he moved towards Gangasagar where the Ganga meets the sea Bay of Bengal. After the pious bathing in the water of the sea he again returned to Mathura-Vrindavan.

Some also guess that Nityananda here got the information of Harinaam Movement led by Mahaprabhu Sri Gouranga in Nabadwip.

From twelve to thirty two during these twenty years Nityananda roamed out and out alone or sometime with some known or unknown teams of Sannyasis, sometime without food, shelter, medicine whatever were considered the minimum need for livelihood of a man all over the Country. Here, while playing with the children in the water of Kalindi or in the forest of Vrindavan he got the confirmed news that the Samkirtan Movement has got impetuous with its peak. He felt his call is there.

Nityananda jaanilen Prabhur prakash,
Ye abadhi laagi korey Vrindavaney baas,

Jania aaila jhaat Nabadwip purey,
Aasiaa bosilen Nandan Acharyer gharey. –

Nityananda knew the Mahaprabhu's appearance. He was waiting for this movement and without any delay he came to Nabadwip town and took shelter in the house of Nandan Acharya. (29)

3

Nityananda Prabhu Joins the Team

At Nandan Acharya's house

Nityananda came to Nabadwip and took shelter at Nandan Acharya's house. On the other hand, Mahaprabhu Sri Gouranga understanding his presence sent his associates Sribaas and Haridas but they could not find. At last, Mahaprabhu Gourangadev with all associates Himself reached the house of Nandan Acharya direct and found Nityananda as Abadhut Sannyasi like dress with blue colour.

Sov loia Prabhu Nandan Acharyaer ghar,
Jaania uthilaa giya Sri Gourasundar. – Alongwith all the associates Mahaprabhu came over to the house of Nandan Acharya direct. (30)

He found Nityananda seated erect at the portico of the house. Both of them looked at each other. For a few moments, none could speak a single word.

Both Mahaprabhu Sri Gouranga and Nityananda looked at each other without any word. All understood a bold personality has come to serve and protect Mahaprabhu. (31)

Sloka of the Bhagawata recited by Sribaas

Mahaprabhu Sri Gouranga requested Sribaas Acharya and Sri Gadadhar to find a way so that the Person seated in Nandan Acharya's house could be recognized. Sribaas started to recite from the Bhagawat as:-

BarhapeedangNatabarabopuh Karnao Karnikaram

Bibhradwasah Kanaka Kapishang Boijyantishna Maalaam.

Randhraan benordharasudhaya purayan Gopavrindeir

Vrindaranyang swapadaramanag praabishad Geetakirtih.(32)

All listened to Sribaas as Raja Parikshit listened to Sukhdeva. They saw in the eyes of their minds that with other Gopa friends Sri Krishna is entering into the forest in Vrindavan. At His each step, at the each movement of the Divine Body there remains poetic rhythm. Actually, the Divine Body Itself is the presence of all rhythms. He is the best among the actors. He is like a Divine Gandharva. Pea-cock's feathers have decorated His head. Two yellow earrings are reflecting the light of gold. He is dressed in yellow colour. A Voijayanti garland is dangling around His neck. He is pouring nectar of His Divine lips into the Divine flute and the celestial sound is spreading all over the Universe. The Gopa companions are singing the songs of the Glory of Lord Sri Krishna. His Divine footsteps are making the forest in Vrindavan a pious and beautiful place worth to worship even by Heaven and Baikuntha.

Reaction of Nityanandaprabhu

Nityananda with all present visualised this Divine Scene in the eyes of minds and became overwhelmed in love for Lord Sri Krishna and fainted.

Sunimaatra Nityananda sloka uchcharan,
Parilaa murchchhita hoian nahika chetan. – On hearing the sloka Nityananda fainted in love for God. (33)

The stout body tall and sun-tanned fair complexion Nityananda with tears in eyes for Lord Sri Krishna made Gourangadev confident that this person's shoulder would be the right choice of spreading the name of Sri Krishna among all the people irrespective of castes and colors.

Two Incidences Likewise

Let us remember similar incidences in cases of exposure at first meeting of Ishwarpuri and Pundarik Vidyanidhi to devotees in Nabadwip.

1. Ishwarpuri in disguise

We can recollect that once before the initiation of Sri Gouranga Mahaprabhu Ishwarpuri arrived in Nabadwip in disguise. Only Sri Gouranga in the Vidyavilaas period came across Sri Ishwarpuri on the road and could recognize him. But others, even Adwaitacharya at first sight could not recognize Sri Ishwarpuri. Gadadhar and Mukunda then were present there. To see his dilemma Mukunda sang a sing with his God-gifted melodious voice that made Sri Ishwarpuri overwhelmed and both Adwaitacharya and Sri Ishwarpuri embraced each other that both were disciples of great Madhabendrapuri.

2. Pundarik Vidyanidhi's Joining into the Movement

We can also recollect the almost same incidence that happened to Pundarik Vidyanidhi, a disciple of Madhabendrapuri. Gadadhar Pundit met him first in Nabadwip with Mukunda. Vidyanidhi was seated on a luxurious seat encircled with many luxurious materials with Divine fragrances all around and at first sight it was not easy for anybody to recognize him as a true Vaishnav. In order to make sure Gadadhar that Vidyanidhi although chose to lead a luxurious life was a real Vaishnava, Mukunda sang a song on Sri Krishna's giving a moment's respect for a mother to Putana. With this song sang melodiouslyby Mukunda Vidyanidhi was overwhelmed with devotion to Lord Sri Krishna and forgot all the earthly luxurious materials around him. He started to sing and dance with Mukunda's song. All the luxurious materials were destroyed or damaged with his dancing in joy for Lord Sri Krishna. At last, Vidyanidhi fainted on the floor. (34)

We know, at this Gadadhar Pundit was so impressed about deep devotion for Lord Sri Krishna Sri Pundarik Vidyanidhi possessed Gadadhar got sorrow for his misunderstanding at first sight. He opted initiation mantra from Sri Pundarik Vidyanidhi and later Sri Gourangadev approved the dicision.

Pundarik is also another name of Lord Sri Krishna. In samkirtan at Sribaas's house Sri Gouranga Mahaprabhu sometime shouted the name 'Pundarik' 'Pundarik' and the present associates thought it was for His Love for God. But Mahaprabhu Sri Gouranga was also waiting for someone Pundarik who could come from Chittagong. Pundarik Vidyanidhi himself came on foot to Mahaprabhu. Both of them embraced each other and for sometime sang, danced and cried in love for Lord Sri Krishna. Having got a real Vaishnav in the Team of Samkirtan it got more enriched with full strength.

Nityananda danced for love for Lord Sri Krishna

With the reaction of Sribaas's recitation from the Bhagawata, Nityananda danced for love for Lord Sri Krishna and all present at Nandan Acharya's house including Sri Gourangadev danced for love for Lord Sri Krishna. Nityananda floated in happiness in love for Sri Krishna. Sri Gourangadev took Nityananda in his lap (35) although it was heavier for Sri Gourangadev to bear the load of the strong and stout body and twelve years' older Nityananda. To see this situation everybody got pleasure on it.

Sri Baas told-we worship Hari and Hara (Shiva Mahadeva) so, we can follow this little.'

Gadadhar Pundit described the situation as the union of Sri Ramchandra and Sri Lakshman. (36)

Nityananda as Lakshman or Balaram

Some said –there remain only differences of names. They are Sri Ram and Sri Lakshman or Sri Krishna and Sri Balaram. They are the two brothers of all the ages.

Some guessed one must be Sri Krishna and the another must be Arjuna.

The two talked little but remained to look at each other and perhaps they talked through their Divine eyes. (37)

Sri Gouranga Mahaprabhu got immense joy to find Nityananda at Nandan Acharya's house as He was waiting for some one to come. He has also seen in a dream that a strong and stout body with two long hands hanging from the strong and wide shoulders and with eyes full with tears for Lord Sri Krishna has descended from a Divine chariot at the door. Now the person Nityananda has arrived.

Nityanandaprabhu, has been considered, as elder brother of Sri Krishna, Balaram the Bosudeva-Rohini son brought up at Nanda Raja's house. After all Nityanandaprabhu joined the Team of Harinaam Movememnt. (38)

4

Sribaas Angan

Harinaam Movement

Encircling Sri Gouranga Mahaprabhu through day and night, all the devotees and associates spend their time by singing and dancing in the name of Lord Sri Krishna. With the inclusion of Sri Nityananda the Harinaam Movement got its peak. Every participant keeping the memory in heart of the 'entwined in bliss' the eternal yugal Radhakrishna sings and plays musical instruments in Samkirtan. The main door remains closed for outsiders so that non-devotee cannot misinterpret the facts and all the happenings. Sometime, while engaged in madly singing and dancing may not take care of their own clothes, sometime they fall one on another. The scene of extreme pleasure of Kirtan and Nartan everybody loses normal senses. (39)

Sometime, Mahaprabhu engrossed with the love for Sri Krishna jumps on the Vishnu Seat and establishes the power and strength Nityananda possessed. He sang and danced madly with others in the name of Balaram. Mahaprabhu's pleasure was immeasurable. He sang with all and danced amongst all with love for God and love for all the creations of God. Added cause was Nityananda's joining in the Team. (40)

Vyas pujan by Sri Nityananda

Mahaprabhu Sri Gouranga decided Vyas pujan by newly welcomed Nityananda. Nityananda himself at that night broke his *Kamandalu*, the water pot and the stick indicating the sign of a mendicant Sannyasi. Ramai Pundit in the next morning saw the broken things of the Abadhuta and informed Sribaas. Sribaas sent him to Mahaprabhu Sri Gouranga. Mahaprabhu Sri Gouranga came to the spot and taking the broken stick went to the river Ganga. Others like Sribaas, Gadadhar Pundit and also Nityananda followed Mahaprabhu. Mahaprabhu Sri Gouranga took bath in the Ganga and kept the broken parts in flow of the Ganga.

Abadhuta Nityananda is like a child. He started to swim and some time chased a crocodile in the river. All the spectators from the bank shouted for not to chase the crocodile lest it might harm to him. (41)

At last, Mahaprabhu Sri Gouranga shouted and reminded Nityananda to expedite the bathing for the Vyas pujan time is being over. In the full moon day of Aasharah all mendicants on this day maintain the rites of Vyas pujan. (42)

With the direction of Mahaprabhu Sri Gouranga Sribaas as a priest completed the Vyas pujan and placed a garland with celestial fragrances on the hand of Abadhuta Nityananda. Nityananda without uttering the scheduled mantra as directed by Sribaas looked here and there and finding Mahaprabhu nearer, placed the garland on His neck instead of offering it in the name of Vyas at the pujan place. Seeing this all present were surprised and also approved in joy. (43)

Again,

Nityanandaprabhu visualized six handed Sri Krishna with Sankha, Chakra, Gada, Padma, Sarnga Benu. Next, he saw four handed Sri Krishna in two hands playing the flute and in two hands there remain Conch and the Circle. Then saw two handed Sri Krishna holding the eternal flute on the lips, having dressed in yellow colours on His blackish Body. Nityananda after Vyas Pujan felt himself as Balaram and held a club. (44)

Nityananda fainted with the love for Mahaprabhu Sri Gouranga as well as God Sri Krishna. Mahaprabhu encircled with other associates called Nityananda to wake. (45)

Nityananda Prabhu like Gadadhar Pundit preferred to serve Mahaprabhu Sri Gouranga as a servant. This *Dasya bhav* in Vaishnav philosophy is a great thing.

Goudiya vaishnavite people believe that Sri Gouranga is 'Krishnastu Bhagawan Swayaym'. Nityananda is Balaram and Gadadhar is the Radhashakti.

'Naadaa', Sri Adwaitacharya's coming in the Movement

Mahaprabhu once started to call loudly 'Naadaa, Naadaa' that mean where is Adwaitacharya, 'the Naadaa called Me, and I am incarnated for his repeated callings'. It is fact that Adwaitacharya worshipped daily with Tulsi leaf and the water of the Ganga requesting Lord Sri Krishna for His reappearance in order to establish order in the society. Mahaprabhu Sri Gouranga sent Ramai Pundit to bring him in Nabadwip and advised to narrate that the Samkirtan team is now ready.

Adwaitacharya with his wife and some puja materials arrived in Nabadwip but advised not to disclose his presence to Mahaprabhu. Mahaprabhu Sri Gouranga feeling the presence of Adwaitacharya shouted 'See, Naadaa has come here and he would not wait for a moment'. Actually, Adwaitacharya could not wait for a single moment. With Sitadevi, he came to the house of Sribaas where the Movement got momentum.

Mahaprabhu Sri Gourangadev showed him all the associates and told him – "All you see here are born as a result of your prayer". (46)

Adwaitacharya worshipped Mahaprabhu Sri Gourangadev

Adwaitacharya started to worship nicely decorated by Gadadhar Pundit, Mahaprabhu Sri Gourangadev with Pujan materials and well known mantras . (47)

Engrossed with the love for Sri Krishna Mahaprabhu Sri Gourangadev received Puja and Pranam of elderly Adwaitacharya and Sitadevi with their child

Achyutananda. He directed to participate in the Samkirtan and Adwaitacharya sang and danced for Lord Sri Krishna for sometime.

Nityananda's Childlike behaviour at Sribaas's House

Day after day Nityananda's childlike behahaviour escalated. He remained at Sribaas's residence. Sribaas's wife Malinidevi considered Nityananda as her elder son for his childlike behave.

At every night with Nityananda, Gadadhar, Adwaitacharya, Sribaas, Pundarik Vidyanidhi, Murari, Govinda, Hiranya, Haridas, Gangadas, Bonamali, Vijoynandan, Jagadananda, Buddhimanta Khan, Narayan, Kashiswar, Basudev, Ram, Garurai, Govindananda, Gopinath, Sriman, banana cone seller Sridhar, Sadashiv, Mukunda, Sanjoy, Srigarva, almost mendicant Suklambar Brahmachari, Chandrasekhar and many others Mahaprabhu participates in chanting the name of Lord Sri Krishna.

5

With a Full Team Mahaprabhu's Nabadwiplila

Nityananda Roamed in the Town

Nityananda roamed in the town Nabadwip the whole day and sometime he swims in the Ganga. Sometime plays he with the children here and there. Sometime Nityananda reaches at the houses of other devotees of Lord Sri Krishna. Sometime Nityananda reaches at the house of Mahaprabhu Sri Gourangadev where he found Sachimaa. Sachimaa also found Nityananda in the dress of Abadhut. She took him as her elder son Vishwaroop who left the family forever in search of God. She felt comfort that his only remainig son Nemai now got an elder brother like Nityananda.

Sri Nityananda at Sri Gouranga's House

Sachimaa one day invited Nityananda to their house for lunch. Mahaprabhu Sri Gourangadev cautioned him not to show any childlike restlessness in the house. Touching both the ears as a good boy uttered 'Vishnu',

'Vishnu'. He also said restlessness is for a mad person but he is not mad one. Mahaprabhu laughed loudly but did not speak a word. Laughingly they two Nityananda and Sri Gouranga sat with Gadadhar and others. (48)

Ishan a Blessed Person at Mahaprabhu's House

Ishan remained at Mahaprabhu's house to serve the family so was fortunate that he got the chances of serving Mahaprabhu, Nityananda, Gadadhar and other associates Vaishnavas. (49)

Vishnupriyadevi Witnesses Nityananda's Lila with Mahaprabhu

From behind the door Jaganmata Vishnupriyadevi the wife of Mahaprabhu Sri Gourangadev looked the scene of the lunch taking ceremony where Sri Nityananda, Sri Gourangadev with Sri Gadadhar and some other associates sat on aasana to take Prasad and to talk on various items. Sachimaa was serving the necessary food to them. All including Vishnupriyadevi witnessed some Divine and naked children of age below five are seated on aasanas. There some also saw that a Divine child with fair complexion and a Divine child with dark black colour encircled by other Divine children enjoying the eating.

Sachimaa's Pleasure

To see this celestial accepting of food cooked by her, Sachimaa fainted as she saw Chaturbhuja Narayan among children friends. Mahaprabhu without any comment washing hands lifted mother and took her inside the room.

Nityananda's Vivacity Enhanced

Thus, day after day, Nityananda's vivacity enhanced. Mahaprabhu's glory spread all over Nabadwip.

Mahaprabhu wandered along with Nityananda and Gadadhar Pundit at the houses of Gangadas Pundit, Murari, Chandrasekhar Acharya and many others, including obviously of Sribaas, who worshipped Sri Krishna at the corner of their houses and showed Chaturbhuj and Sadabhuj appearances. Sometime thus with Gadadhar's deep concern and Nityananda's tremendous vivacity for Shri Krishna confounded with the state of mind of each *Avatar* among ten *Avataras* Mahaprabhu Sri Gourangadev sang and danced at Sribaas angan. (50)

Mahaprabhu Sri Gourangadev Possessed by Shiva Mahadeva

Oneday, a songster of Shiva Mahadeva came to the house of Mahaprabhu Sri Gourangadev for begging alms. Mahaprabhu having possessed by Shiva Mahadeva sang and danced with him. He jumped on the shoulder of the songster and cried –I'm Shiva, Soasmi, mui Shiva'. All there assembled to witness the singing and dancing of the songster surprisingly noticed this incidence. Getting back to normal sense Mahaprabhu Sri Gourangadev came down and made the bag of begging full with plenty of things.

Sribaas, Mukunda and Govinda Sang and Danced Around Mahaprabhu

With the direction of Mahaprabhu one team led by Sribaas, one team led by Mukunda having melodious voice, one team led by Govinda Dutta sing around Mahaprabhu. (51)

Mental makeup of others

The people who did not prefer Sri Krishna were afraid of infidel ruler's men of own religion and his administrative people. The Samkirtan Movement may invite unnecessary problem on the peaceful lives and property of ordinary citizens. Ruler's people would not judge who is involved or not. Getting any lame excuse they might destroy and loot lives, women and property and also religion. The people who did not prefer the Samkirtan Movement gossiped that Sribaas who has allowed own house for Kirtan at first he should be thrown out. Not only Sribaas, now another strange and strong personality with full of vivacity Nityananda by name has also joined the whole nightlong Kirtan. This should be stopped without any delay. They started to scandalize that keeping doors closed the participants enjoy earthly materials.

Gopal Chaapaal

One Gopal Chaapaal one day with an intention to tease the Samkirtan Movement originating from Sribaas'a house kept some materials for worshipping goddess Shakti at the door of Sribaas. The person did not understand that Mahaprabhu and the associates had no reservation for any gods or goddesses or for any religions. Rather Lord Sri Krishna, Himself took the help of His Yogamaya Shakti Devi at His exposed birth to Basudeva-Devakee and His bringing up at Nanda–Jashoda's house. The Brajo Gopies used to worship Katyayanidevi to have Lord Sri Krishna. While after giving Mukti to Kansa Basudeva-Devakee could not accept Krishna and Balaram as their sons Sri Krishna also took the help of Maya Shakti by depending on Katyayani and then with the power of Maya their parents accepted Balaram and Krishna as their own children and they behaved accordingly. Even before the eternal Rasa Sri Krishna took the help of His Yogamamya power and then entered into the forest of Vrindavan.

Having found Gopal Chaapaal's audacity Mahaprabhu felt anger. Within three days, that Gopal Chaapaal became a lepor. On the roadside of Mahaprabhu's thoroughfare to the Ganga every morning Gopal Chaapaal begged for mercy but Mahaprabhu replied him to wait and suffer for some days. In the long run, while Mahaprabhu came to Bengal from Puri after vigorous travel in southern part of India forgave the person. Being healed from hatred disease Gopal Chaapaal joined in the enlarged team of Samkirtan. Seeing Mahaprabhu's Divine ability in different aspects all devotees became surprised. (52)

Mahaprabhu Sri Gourangadev's Coronation

Once, all the devotees at Sribaas's house desired to observe a ceremony of Mahaprabhu Sri Gourangadev's coronation. Some brought pitches after pitches of water from the Ganga and poured on Mahaprabhu. Some uttered the Slokas from the Vedas. Some, including Adwaitacharya, worshipped Mahaprabhu with various kinds of Puja materials. Nityananda held the umbrella on Sri Gourangadev's head. Gadadhar Pundit decorated Mahaprabhu with garlands and painted Tilakas with sandal wood paste. Gadadhar Pundit also remained with Pan leaves for Mahaprabhu's chewing. Different teams chanted the songs of Lord Sri Krishna around Mahaprabhu. Mahaprabhu then accepted all the people irrespectively whoever came to Him for a darshan and all participated in the Samkirtan.

Having courage and silent indulgence all started to place *Durba* (one kind of immortal grass), paddy and Tulsi leaves at Mahaprabhu's feet.(53)

Narayani got blessings from Mahaprabhu Sri Gourangadev

Mahaprabhu Sri Gourangadev's love showered on many people of different trades, banana cone seller Sridhar, Shuklambar Brahmachari and many children He came across and a little girl of four Narayani too.

At Sribaas Angan in Nabadwip when Mahaprabhu was engaged with chanting and dancing almost the whole day, one day He found a little girl of about four years' old crying for something. This little girl was Narayani, daughter of Sribaas's deceased eldest brother Nalini. Her crying drew the attention of Lord Sri Gouranga.

Mahaprabhu asked her- "why you are crying maa".

The girl remained silent for a while and again started to cry.

Mahaprabhu then advised her – "If you want to cry, cry for Lord Sri Krishna, utter Sri Krishna. He is the Lord of us. He can give everything if He desires. Cry for Him"

Surprisingly the four years' child started to cry by saying 'Haa Krishna, Krishna, Krishna, Krishna Hey' and tears from her eyes started to fall.

To see it Mahaprabhu was pleased and blessed her. Mahaprabhu gave her the end of food eaten up almost every day while she was in Nabadwip.

Birth of Vrindavandas, the Vyas of Sri Chaitanyalila

Afterwards this Narayani was married to one Brahmin person of Kumarhatta named Baikunthadas. Unfortunately, that Baikuntha expired leaving her pregnant. Sribaas brought this fatherless and husbandless carrying girl to his house at Kumarhatta.

There on Krishnaa dwadashi (12th day of new moon) in 1429 Saka widow Narayani gave birth to a male baby. This baby afterwards became Vrindavandas, the Vyas of Sri Chaitanyalila. He wrote the Sri Chaitanya Bhagawat and still it gives the readers and devotees the maximum information of Nabadwiplila and others of Sri Gouranga Mahaprabhu and His all associates.

6

Nabdwiplila Continues

Malini Devi and Nityananda as Mother and Son

Nityananda's Lila of childlike behaviour continued. Sribaas's wife Malini Devi and Nityananda had a relation of a mother and a son. He did not feel any hesitation to her. Sometime he forgot to wear clothes under the waist. He tied his head with it and sang and danced in the name of Lord Sri Krishna. To see this Sribaas, Gadadhar, Haridas even Sri Gourangadev laughed and advised him to wear own clothes properly. Sri Gouranga Mahaprabhu called him and advised, it is a custom of familymen to wear dresses properly. (54)

Once a crow took away Malini Devi's pot of ghee. Knowing this Nityananda called the crow and the crow gave the pot back. Malinidevi saw the influence of Nityananda. She was surprised and praised him in joy. (55)

Nityananda with Childlike Restlessness at Mahaprabhu's House

One day while Mahaprabhu was at home with Sachimaa and Vishnupriyadevi Sri Nityananda with childlike restlessness came there without any dress. Laughingly Mahaprabhu asked– "Why you are *digambara*? Do put on your clothes." Nityananda did not heed to Mahaprabhu's advice but told mother Sachidevi- "Give me food maa." Nityananda was engrossed with the essence of Gourangadev's love so he could not wear clothes nor could listen to the advice. Mahaprabhu Gourangadev brought a piece of cloth from inside the room and helped him to wear.

Sachimaa considered Nityananda her elder son Vishwaroop so although it was not a time for lunch or dinner she brought five pieces of sweets Sandesh from inside the room and gave those to Nityananda. Nityananda began to dance with the sweets but those dropped on grounds. Sachimaa told him – What you have done Netai. There is no more in our house. What then I should give you?"

Nityananda replied calmly – Maa, I know very well there are more sweets at your possession, see there minutely."

She became surprised to note that truely there at same place were the five sweets but mixed with some dust of grounds. With rubbing all, she again gave to Netai again.

Nityananda said to her - I find your sorrow so I have brought these again". (56)

Sachimaa requested Nityananda – Do not play false with me. I feel that you are God Yourself."

Nityananda tried to touch her feet to show respect but Sachimaa ran into inside. Vishnupriyadevi and Sri Gourangadev got pleasure to see this scene. Nityananda's character is not easily understood. (57)

Sri Gouranga Mahaprabhu expressed the Glory of Nityananda

The character of Nityananda is not easily comprehensible. Excepting some uncommon things, the role of Nityananda Prabhu in the History of Vaishnav Movement in the Country is not easily measurable by ordinary people.

To see such engrossed position in love for Lord Sri Krishna as well as Sri Gouranga Mahaprabhu He reminded Nityananda Prabhu again that, it is not the customs to remain undressedly and to attend at a house of any social family. He brought down his turban from the head and helped to wear it around the waist.

Later Mahaprabhu tore one of his under short garment and distributed the pieces to other associates and advised all to wear the pieces of the cloth on their heads so that all get Sri Krishnabhakti. Mahaprabhu also arranged Nityananda's Charanamrita for others for the same purpose. He again advised all to wash Nityananda's feet knowing the full power of God in Nityananda. (58)

But, Nityananda remained same dashing-pushing personality with full of vivacity and participated in the Samkirtan and danced alongwith Sri Gouranga

Mahaprabhu. Other associates sang and danced in joy encircling the Divine twins.

The purpose of the Samkirtan of Mahaprabhu

Mahaprabhu's intention was to enlarge the Movement of Samkirtan not for only religious purpose but also to mend the Society. If everybody feel interested in the Samkirtan and gather under an umbrella, from the society all evil and bad things would disappear. Man would get proper respect of a man from the others.

One day Mahaprabhu advised Nityananda and Haridas to distribute Harinaam among the people of Nabadwip.

Suno suno Nityananda suna Haridas,
Sarbatra aamar agya karaha prachar,
Prati gharey gharey ei kara giya viksha,
Krishna Bhaja, Krishna bola, kara Krishna siksha.(59)

They from dawn to dust started to tell everyone in the town to worship Lord Sri Krishna and many people responded to their preachings.

Jagai-Madhai

Unfortunately, there were two Brahmin young men at the charge of controlling administration on behalf of the ruler remained always drunk and did not prefer them. One day having drunk much they were weltering on the middle of roads. Nityananda and Haridas, despite other gentlemen's caution not to go to them, they went to their nearer and started to sing-

Bolo Krishna, bhajo Krishna, kaho Krishna naam,

Krishna mata Krishna pita Krishna dhana prana.(60)

The drunken kotwals chased them but could not catch. Haridas and Nityananda at last arrived at Sribaas's house and thus they could escape.

An out post was established on the way of the ghat of the Ganga. There remain the two drunk Jagai and Madhai. Again on another day Nityananda and Haridas arrived where the two drunk Kotwals were weltering in toxicated position. They both started to sing Harinaam but the drunk Madhai knowing the name of Nityananda without any delay struck on Nityananda's head with an emptied pot of drinks. Blood shed from Nityananda's head. To see it Jagai rebuked Madhai that it was much.

Having heard this Mahaprabhu with the associates came to the spot and found Nityananda in bleeding situation is laughing Divinely. Being angry enough He said - Nityananda is bigger than me and you dared to cause his bleeding". All the associates saw that Mahaprabh is holding the Chakra up. (61)

Nityananda finding Mahaprabhu's anger requested Mahaprabhu to be calm and himself begged the lives of Jagai and Madhai. Mahaprabhu returning to normalcy told him – I can forgive Jagai but Madhai has to pray pardon to Nityananda as he hurt him". Madhai did so. Sri Nityananda embraced Madhai and Jagai. The two brothers in love for them became senseless. The devotees carried them at Mahaprabhu's house.

At own residence, Mahaprabhu seated taking Nityananda at the right and Gadadhar at the left,

Adwaitacharya at the fore, others like Pundarik Vidyanidhi, Haridas, Garurai Ramai, Sribaas, Gangadas, Bakreswar Pundit, Chandrasekhar acharya, and all of the associates around forgave the two brothers in the Samkirtan. (62)

Jagai and Madhai started to praise the glories of Sri Gouranga Mahaprabhu, Sri Nityananda, Sri Gadadhar, Sribaas, Sri Adwaitacharya and other Vaishnavas. They surprisingly used the words as if Devi Saraswati Herself has seated on their tongues. They, thus became a part and parcel of the Harinaam Movement. Sachimaa and Vishnupriyadevi witnessed this Historical incidence. It touched all of the people of Nabadwip.

Jalkeli at the time of bathing in the Ganga

Every morning after whole night Samkirtan at the time of bathing in the Ganga with Sri Gouranga Mahaprabhu Adwaitacharya, Nityananda, Gadadhar, Sribaas, Haridas and others Vaishnavas passed time like children. Mahaprabhu inspires all of them to play Jalkeli.

Repentation of Jagai and Madhai and Correction

Jagai – Madhai being whole-heartedly Vaishnav could not forget that once they had assaulted Nityananda and Haridas and grimaced the Samkirtan. They always remain morosed. One day Madhai got Nityananda alone and expressed his sorrow. Nityananda advised him to keep clean and decorate the ghat on the Ganga that Mahaprabhu uses for bathing with all other devotees regularly. Madhai did so and began to offer due respect to the people who used the ghat for bathing. The ghat was known as Madhaiyer ghat.

Once Mahaprabhu felt uncomfortable in Samkirtan

One day during Samkirtan Mahaprabhu felt there is something wrong in the house. There must be any unauthorized person in the Samkirtan but every body present was known to each other. Sribaas searched every corner and found his mother-in-law who did not prefer Harinaam Movement. Sribaas politely advised her to leave the place and to come later. Nobody knew this but Mahaprabhu again got enthusiasm in the Samkirtan with other Vaishnavas.

Respect exchanged between Adwaitacharya and Mahaprabhu

On another day, Mahaparbhu fainted in love for Lord Sri Krishna. Getting a scope to have a Pranam Adwaitacharya touched Mahaprabhu's feet and took the dust and rubbed it on his own body. He took Sri Gouranga Mahaprabhu as Lord Sri Krishna. Mahaprabhu naturally could not know it but Mahaprabhu did not get so much enthusiasm in Samkirtan. He within a few moments understood the reason and started to talk much with Adwaitacharya. Adwaitacharya was singing and dancing that he has received the valuable dust of Mahaprabhu's feet. In the singing and dancing, Mahaprabhu Sri Gourangadev forcibly rubbed repeatedly His own head at the feet of Adwaitacharya. He said, - you have stolen, I can also rob on thieves and laughed". (63)

Mahaprabhu blessed Shuklambar Brahmachari

The Samkirtan Movement became popular day by day with the presence of all the devotees of Lord Sri Krishna. One day there came Shuklambar Brahmachari and joined the team. Mahaprabhu found him to sing and dance with others. He was dancing and his belonging a bag full of begged rice of various quality was also swinging. Mahaprabhu took some handful of rice and particles and started to chew. (64)

7

Drama, an Instrument of Propaganda

Drama Lakshmikaach (some say the name of the Drama was RUKMINI SAMBAD) (Mahaprabhu as Dramatist, Composer and Director)

Mahaprabhu Sri Gourangadev knew that acting of Drama is an instrument of propaganda. At that time, there were no Newspaper nor Radio nor Television nor any kind of Media. It was most essential to circulate the news of Harinaam Movement throughout the Country. There was no other way than to sing and staging a drama. However, people irrespective of castes, languages, culture and even religion are to be united under a common umbrella. He therefore, decided to perform a drama written on the stage spontaneously with all his associates. The drama was Lakshmikaach composed by words after words by Mahaprabhu Himself. Some say that the name of the Drama was Rukmini Sambad.

Buddhimanta Khan the Producer and Manager

Buddhimanta Khan, a well to do and having some experience of stage and costumes for a stage drama arranged different costumes and essential materials and erected a stage in the open space at the house of Chandrasekhar Acharya.

At the initial Mukunda, Ramkrishna, Narahari, Gopal, Govinda and others participated in the Kritan.

Haridas as the Curtain Raiser

In the first act, dressed in costumes entered as joiner to recite the prologue. He announced himself as the Kotwal the chief of the administration of the Baikuntha.

Mahaprabhu as actor in female costumes

Gadadhar Pundit was to act as Rukmini. However, being absorbed in emotion for Lord Sri Krishna Sri Gouranga Mahaprabhu Himself appeared in the dress of Rukmini. In the drama, Rukmini is writing a letter to Sri Krishna for his coming to her and to rescue her before Sishupal comes to marry her. She is earnestly requesting Sri Krishna to save her from the hands of Sishupal. Mahaprabhu becomes absorbed in the emotion. Rukmini was devoted to Lord Sri Krishna throughout all her lives. Rukmini is also considered as Lakshmi in Puranas.

Gadadhar Pundit in female costumes (Hladini' power Srimati Radharani)

Gadahar Pundit is considered as 'Hladini' power Srimati Radharani who supplies joy to Sri Krishna continuously. In the Second Act, Gadadhar in the dress of Roma (Lakshmi, Radharani), entered on the stage with one companion in the dress of Subhadra sister of Sri

Krishna. Drama continued in full swing. Thereafter, Gadadhar danced as Roma the wife of Lord Narayan. Having nice look Gadadhar with fine make-up with ornaments and richly dress could easily steal the hearts of the audience. All felt Gadadhar is the Lakshmi the eternal wife of Lord Narayana, Sri Krishna. With the love for Sri Krishna the tears of Gadadhar drenched the earth, really Gadadhar was the 'Hladini' power of Lord Sri Krishna. (65)

Here the reality of the Drama and the truth of the belief are mixed. Gadadhar is the 'Hladini' power Radharani of Lord Sri Krishna In the past ages of the eternity.

Adwaitacharya appeared on the stage in disguise. Sribaas dressed with white beard, having a *Veena*, a musical instrument made of strings on the shoulder and a *koosh aasana* in hand appeared as Narada. Malinidevi the wife of Sribaas could not recognize her husband. Each actor was so expertly dressed as the character of the drama that all the spectators of the audience although all came from their own houses could not easily recognize own men.

Mahaprabhu as the Adya Shakti, Nityananda as Badaai

Mhaprabhu Sri Gouranga appeared as the Adya Shakti. No one could recognize the actor. He was so expert in acting. Nityanada Prabhu acted as Mahaprabhu's Badaai. No one could recognize Him before the last scene. (66)

Prayer to Adya Shaktidevi Mahaprabhu in acting

Among the spectators some thought Mahaprabhu as Lakshmi, some as Sitadevi, some as Parvatidevi, some as the Vrindavaneswari Radharani. Some of them also took as the Bhagirathi, some as Daya, and some as the Mahamaya. Mahaparbhu thus explained to the spectators that there is no difference between Shakti and Sri Krishna. Mahaprabhu in the dress of Adya Shaktidevi appeared to Rukmini. To see this, even Sachimaa could not realize that her son is acting as Adya Shakti. (67)

Mahaprabhu as the Esternal Mother of the Universe

Mahaprabhu danced as the goddess Bhakti and sat on a khatta (a seat made of wood) and showed the Mahalakshmi appearance. All there, started to worship with the slokas they knew for worshipping Shakti Devi at their houses. Here Mahaprabhu is as the eternal Mother of the Universe.

8

On the Streets of Nabadwip

At the houses of all devotees

The news of Mahaprabhu's Harinaam Movement spread all over Bengal. With other associates, hladini shakti Gadadhar Pundit and elder brother Balaram like Nityananda Prabhu. He traveled at the houses of all devotees in Nabadwip. (68)

On way to Shantipur

Mahaprabhu Sri Gourangadev always remained in tremendous excitement of passion in love for Lord Sri Krishna. During this period, Mahaprabhu opined to meet Adwaitacharya as for a few days he was not getting him. He with Nityananda started to walk along the Ganga towards Shantipur.

On their way, they came to a village Lalitpur and found a beautiful house with full of various flowers. It was mid day and they chose the house for taking a little rest.

One Shakti devotee

The house owner was an elderly devotee of Shakti. The Sadhak finding Nityananda and Mahaprabhu expressed his happiness. They both offered due respect to him. In return he gave them blessing saying - Be happy with money, learnings and beautiful wife".

Mahaprabhu calmly said to him – No, no it is not good blessing, you could say that we should have strong attachment for Sri Krishna. Vishnubhakti is imperishable".

The Sannyasi laughed and blamed that he wanted to do good for them but they did not understand it. Mahaprabhu raised his long hands and replied – All earthly materials are perishable but strong attachment to Sri Krishna is permanent and it continues even after death. Moreover, it gives everything whatever one needs." The Sannyasi did not prefer this learning from juniors like Mahaprabhu and Nityananda. However, Nityananda managed the situation and the Sannyasi requested them to take bath as their food was ready.

After bath in the Ganga they sat for taking fruits, sweets etc. The Sannyasi expressed in gesture that he had more material for enjoyment in his stock. His wife from behind the doors tried to control but could not. Nityananda had practical experience of outer world so he from the first sight could recognize the character of the Sannyasi. Mahaprabhu just uttered 'Vishnu, Vishnu' and started to walk with Nityananda.

Knowledge and Devotion

They swum in the Ganga and arrived at Adwaitacharya's house. Seeing to read something attentively Mahaprabhu asked Adwaitacharya some questions about Knowledge and Devotion but his reply did not satisfy Mahaprabhu Sri Gourangadev. He pulled down the old man and was about to beat but Sitadevi came and saved her husband. Child Achyutananda and Mahaprbhu's most beloved Haridas also came there. Ultimately both Mahaprabhu Sri Gourangadev and Adwaitacharya embraced each other. (69)

At Adwaitacharya's house Nityananda as a child

At the end of taking lunch at Adwaitacharya's house Nityananda scattered some rice here and there. To see this abnormal behaviour Haridas just could laugh, Mahaprabhu tried to control but Adwaitacharya was offended. They both started to continue quarrels of pleasure.

Murari Gupta

At Sribaas's house in Nabadwip one day Murari Gupta came and showed due respect to Mahaprabhu at first, then to Nityananda. Mahaprabhu advised Murari Gupta to go back to his place. Later Murari realized from a dream that he should offer Pranam at first to senior one Nityananda but he did not maintain the social customs. On the second day Murari Gupta did accordingly.

Murari Gupta had the family profession of treating ailments; so sometime he helped Mahaprabhu and others from ailment. He was a follower of Sri Ramchandra. He once wished to commit suicide remembering the pain for sorrows Sitadevi had during her captivity by Ravana. He also thought that Lord Sri Krishna Himself became a prey with the arrow of a hunter. Oh, it cannot be imagined. In sorrow of the incidences of the past Murari brought a kind of chopper and kept it at a hiding place in his dwelling room. It was a great fortune that Mahaprabhu understood it and hurriedly arrived at Murrai's house and Himself brought out the sharp weapon back from the hiding place.

He said - Give me your body. You are not the proprietor of the body. If you surrender it to me you would have no right on it". Saying this took his hands and placing on own head Mahaprabhu said – Give me words. You would never do such wrong in life".

Leaving such affection he wanted to commit suicide? Murari, thinking so, burst into tears and fell at the feet of Mahaprabhu.

Sukriti Murari kandey dhariya charan,
Gupta koley kori kandey Sachira Nandan.(70)

Gadadhar Pundit used to decorate Sri Gourangadev Everyday

Mahprbhu's life long companion Gadadhar Pundit every day used to decorate Mahaprabhu Sri Gourangadev with garlands, Tilak of Sandle wood pastes and Mahaprabhu roamed in the town of Nabadwip. It was a regular routine for a period of few months of His roaming in the places where people of different trades and culture inhabited.

Unity and Integrity the Country needs

Nityananda all the time preferred to serve and remain with Sri Gourangadev. Nityananda's life Sri Gourasundar, Gadadhar's Lord Sri Gourasundara, Adwaita's Sri Gouranga, causing pleasure to Sribaas Haridas's Sri Gouranga, God of Gangadas, Basudev's

Mahaprabhu Sri Gouranga; thus attracted all in Nabadwip. The Country needs unity and integrity, so all are to come under a systematic umbrella otherwise the Country would not breathe peacefully. Mahaprabhu Sri Gourangadev considered that if all categories of people can unite themselves in good causes and try to maintain the integrity among themselves the maximum problems of Mankind would disappear. Therefore, Mahaprabhu roamed here and there to inspire all in a common platform. For Him then it was the Harinaam Movement.

Mahaprabhu with Nityananda and Gadadhar in Nabadwip

Mahaprabhu with Nityananda and Gadadhar roamed in the town of Nabadwip. It became a regular routine of His roaming in the places where people of different trades and culture assemble or inhabit. Mahaprabhu always preferred to be painted and duly decorated in the hands of beloved Gadadhar Pundit. (71)

Mahaprabhu felt uncomfortable again at Sribaas angan

One day at Sribaas angan Mahaprabhu could feel something was wrong in the Samkirtan. There, one sincere worshipper of other god/goddess with taking permission from Sribaas remained inside to witness the Samkirtan. Sri Gourangadev unknowing it asked, if there was any unauthorized person. Sribaas admitted. Mahaprabhu cautioned that, a only mere devotee, how much sincere he is, without having unconditional faith and devotion (Bhakti) to Sri Krishna is not authorised for attending the Samkirtan. That brahmachari came up and bowed his head under the Divine feet of Mahaprabhu and in Bhakti he started to chant and dance with all.

Bhakti must be in interpretation of the Srimad Bhagawata

Like wise Mahaprabhu advised Devananda Pundit, a renowned interpreter of the Srimad Bhagawat, that without Bhakti in Lord Sri Krishna interpretation is useless. Without Bhakti the listeteners may mean the interpretation of the Bhagawat as of activities of ordinary men and women with earthly flesh and blood not as divinely and supernatural activities of Lord Sri Krishna. He said as a scripture the Srimadbhagawat is also Sri Krishna.

Chaari Veda dadhi nabaneet,

Mathilen Sukey khailen Parikshit. As if four Vedas are like curds, cream etc. Sukhdev Goswami stirred and made a palatable dish and Raja Parikshit tasted it.(72)

Mahaprabhu advised all the people 'Harinaam'

Now Mahaprabhu advised all the people assembled there at Sribaas Angan to utter loudly or silently or on rosary the Mahamantra –

Hare Krishna Hare Krishna Krishna Krishna Hare Hare

Hare Rama Hare Rama Rama Rama Hare Hare.(73)

He advised all to chant the Mahamantra along with all the members of the family everyday with whatever instruments are available at their homes or by clapping. The advice is considered as the Initiation Mantra given by Mahaprabhu. He also advised to sing –

Harayey Namah Krishna Jadavaya Namah,
Gopala Govinda Rama Sri Madhusudana.(74)

9

The Triumphant Democratic Rally Against Kazi and Nabadwiplila Matures

Local Kazi Banned the Samkirtan

One day local Kazi, a representative of ruler Hussain Shah of Goud Bengal somehow could hear that some people are engaged in Samkirtan loudly with some musical instruments. He also received the information from the people who opposed Mahaprabhu's Samkirtan Movement and sometime created disturbances. Although having different belief Kazi at primary level did not interfere in the Samkirtan Movement. However being provoked by a few people of Nabadwip naturally Kazi agreed to take necessary action and ultimately passed orders to ban the Harinaam Movement.

Kazi's people broke the musical instruments (Khole-Mridanga etc.). They also cautioned all not to chant loudly any longer in the Nabadwip.

Mahapranju hearing this ban became furious and gave a Call to all to unite to fight against it. Calmly He made some groups with one chief. At the front Adwaitacharya would lead a team. In the middle Haridas would lead the team of singers. Then Sribaas would lead a team of Kirtaniyas. And then Mahaprabh Sri Gourangadev with Nityananda at his choice at the right side and Gadadhar Pundit at the left side lead with a team of singers.

Nityananda said boldly –I shall be with you all along. Yatha tumi tatha aami ei mora bhakti – (75)

The Team of Rally

In the procession of Samkirtan, there were more like Bakreswar, Murari, Gopinath, Jagadish, Bipra Gangadas, Ramai Pundit, Govindananda, Sri Chandrasekhar, Basudev, Sri Garva, Mukunda, Sri Dhar, Govinda, Jagadananda, Nandan Acharya, Suklambar Brahmachari and other Vaishnavas. Thousands of ordinary people irrespective of castes and rich and poor, Vaishnav or not whoever heard Kazi's banning on the Samkirtan started to join in the long Rally of Protest.

After the sunset Mahaprabhu at fist started to sing

Harayey Namah Krishna Jadavaya Namah,
Gopala Govinda Rama Sri Madhusudana.

Under the black sky with twinkling stars, thousands of devotees and people of different sections of the society resounded in the Kirtan. Thousands of burning torches were in the hands of the people. All with garlands around their necks, with their respective signs of Tilak on the forehead and at more eleven places on whole body started to sing and dance around Mahaprabhu. Then Sri Gourangadev started to move and the ocean of men followed Mahaprabhu towards the village Simulia where Kazi resided. On the way throughout different roads and lanes people joined the moving rally and made it more longer at every advancement. Women at their nicely decorated doors with flowers and leaves of mango tree greeted the rally showering with flowers, offering garlands and sounding mangal Hulu (sound made by women). Having a Divine look nicely dressed of Sri Gouranga Mahaprabhu, Nityananda, Gadadhar and all others singing and dancing devotees and followers associates of Mahaprabhu all were contented.

The colourful rally was marching along the Ganga, the streets, the localities with dance and songs like -

Harayey Namah Krishna Jadavaya Namah,

Gopala Govinda Rama Sri Madhusudana.

One group sang-

Tuaar charaney mon laaguhurey,

Sarngadhara tuaar charaney mon laaguhurey.

Another group sang-

Haribol mugdha Govinda Bolrey,

Yaha hoitey naahi hoi shaman bhoyrey.

Some of Kirtaniyas sang-

Vijoy hoilaa Hari Nandaghosera bala,

Hari Hari haathey bansi goley banamala.(76)

At Kazi's dwelling house

Mahaprabhu at last with the mammoth rally reached the village Simulia at Kazi's dwelling house. Thousands of people, associates and the Kirtaniyas followed Mahaprabhu. Many of the people were madly in dancing and singing and jumping-kicking. Some were uncontrollable too. Kazi went in hiding in fear of the power of the mass. Some uncontrollable participants messed up flower gardens, roofs of the rooms but Mahaprabhu rudely ordered them to stop and He with the help of a few modest and gentle company called Kazi from inside the house. (77)

Kazi sat on his seat in front Mahaprabhu. Kazi informed Sri Gouranga that Sri Gouranga was his beloved nephew in relation of Village. Mahaprabhu admitted it as this kind of relation according to village with people of different religions was in vogue in Bengal. Same friendly relation till date are also in vogue in the lives of people of the country. They both discussed on philosophical aspects of respective Religions.

Having witnessed the power of the mass and convincing words of Mahaprabhu at last Kazi was convinced. Having admitted the right of Samkirtan, Kazi ultimately was bound to withdraw the orders of banning Samkirtan.

Thus openly chanting 'Kirtan' got license from the Ruling Authority. Hearing this confession and the permanent permission thousands of united voices arose with triumphant sound and made the sky of Nabadwip full with this. The Human Right as well as Social and the Religious right thus was established by a part of the Ruling Authority. (78)

News of this movement without any arms but only with songs and dances in the name of Lord Sri Krishna and led by Lord Gouranga Mahaprabhu reached other places of the Country.

Mahaprabhu with the followers hoisting the victorious flag and the sign of 'Panja' walked with Kirtan on the streets.

The Triumphant Rally returned through the places of the citizens

Then Mahaprabhu travelled at Gadigachha, Payraadaanga, and other localities with all the associates and the people who joined in the Historical Rally. All showered flowers on Mahaprabhu and others. Being much more engrossed with love for Lord Sri Krishna that Mahaprabhu Sri Gourangadev even drank water in the broken iron pot left at the corner of the house of Sridhar.

10

People Coming under Harinaam Umbrella

Nabadwip Lila is in Saturation

Now Nabadwip Lila is in a matured stage but the name of Lord Sri Krishna should be spread over rest of the vast Country. The Krishna naam movement has wiped out the caste system and other differences among the ordinary people. People cite Kirtan all along and regained self-confidence. They can believe that they are men. This self-respect gave them tremendous enthusiasm of being active in all spheres of lives. So sizeable changes were observed everywhere even in the fields of cultivation and small industry and especially in the fields of literature. People learnt to work in hand and to utter the name of Lord Sri Krishna on lips. They became so contended that they knew to live happily.

Now it is time to go forward with the name of Lord Sri Krishna. He advised the masses to pray silently or on rosary. He had advised all of His followers and the people to chant the Mahamantra "Hare Krishna Hare Krishna Krishna Krishna Hare Hare, Hare Rama Hare Rama Rama Rama Hare Hare" with whatever musical instruments they had at hand at home for prayer silently or on rosary:

'Atma' or 'Jibatma' in everyone

Mahaprabhu cannot sit idle at home or with lovely wife and to maintain family only by the profession of teaching at school. He is to do more for Lord Sri Krishna. He is to see other places and contact with people at various places in the Country. He is to do more things for the society. He is to lead all to wipe out caste system from the Country. He is to preach everyone that each man is same, as everyone possesses 'Atma' or 'Jibatma' an atomic particle of God the 'Paramatma'.

Mahaprabhu's love for everyone

Mahaprabhu's love for Lord Sri Krishna day after enhanced than that of previous time Mahaprabhu had.

Nityananda matta sinha sarba Nadiayay,

Gharey gharey buley Prabhu anantalilaayay,

Prabhu sangey Gadadhar thaaken sarbthaa,

Adwaita loiyaa sarva Vaishnevera katha - Being inspired Nityananda moved to houses of the people and described Mahaprabhu's unending Lilas. Gadadhar remains with Mahaprabhu all the time. This with Adwait is the subject of all Vaishnavas.(79)

One day on Adwaitacharya's request Mahaprabhu showed the Vishwaroop Murti that once showed Sri Krishna to Arjuna in the Mahabharatiya War, once to maa Yasodha when Sri Krishna did Lila of a child and also once after universal annihilation as Bal Mukunda He showed Markendeya Rishi the whole of the Universe in Him. Adwaitacharya confirmed himself that Mahaprabhu was Himself God Sri Krishna. Nityananda knew it. Gadadhar believed this from the beginning of their lives.

Mahaprabhu all the time was engrossed with the love for Lord Sri Krishna. In Sribaas's house after Samkirtan for Lord Sri Krishna Adwaitacharya and Nityananda engaged themselves in sweet quarrel.

Dukhi became Sukhi

One day there all started to bathe Mahaprabhu with pots after pots of water. One maid servant assisted the followers by bringing huge amount of water from the Ganga. To see much quantity of water supply Mahaprabhu knew the source that a little girl was bringing water from the Ganga. Mahaprabhu asked the name of the girl.

She replied – Dukhi my name is" in low voice.

Mahaprabhu answered – No, it can't be your name as sorrow. You are serving for the Vaishnavas and you deserve the name of a happy girl. You must be happy. Let be your name Sukhi". Since all started to call her Sukhi. We may be sure that getting boon from Mahaprabhu the girl once became happy.

On Sribaas's son's sudden demise

Sribaas's tender aged son suddenly expired but he did not dare to inform fully engrossed in love for Sri

Krishna Mahaprabhu for more than eight hours. At last he approached Mahaprabhu for taking permission of cremation. Mahaprabhu became surprised to note that everybody of the family remained silent so long time only for their unthinkable love they had for Mahaprabhu. Mahaprabhu visited the dead body and asked – why you are leaving this house and all with Sribaas?"

All the associates saw the boy to answer – My time is over here. It is my fate only. So, let me go.

Mahaprabhu Sri Gourangadev consoled Sribaas not to get disappointed. He may consider Nityananda and Mahaprabhu as his two sons.

Aami Nityananda dui nandan tomaar,
Chittey tumi byatha kichhu naa bhaabiha aar.(80)

Naturally, Mahaprabhu had thoughts for hard reality for a family, especially the parents who lost their only child. So Mahaprabhu consoled him that Nityananda who took Malinidevi as mother and He himself assured to be his son.

We can recollect that Mahaprabhu tried to keep His consoling words given to Sribaas. Later once at the house of Sribaas at Kumarhatta Mahaprabhu found that Sribaas is running family in acute hardship because he never begged for himself nor he used to go to disciples' houses in order to earn. Therefore, he had no way to earn only for hand to mouth. He always used to worship Lord Sri Krishna and think of the eternal Lila and those of Mahaprabhu. Sri Gourangadev said to him that without asking for no one offers a single leaf from a tree. Sribaas had no time or intention to go outside for earning. Mahaprabhu realized it and advised his brothers Ramai and others including some devotees to look after this aspect so that Sribaas can maintain the family without any anxiety and then he would be able to think of Lord Sri Krishna. All took it as granted and tried to maintain it.

Worshipping of Sri Vishnu

Being possessed in Smaranam Mahaprabhu could not Worship Sri Vishnu alone. One day Sri Gourangadev decided to worship Sri Vishnu at the house of Sribaas. Sribaas made all arrangements. Mahaprabhu sat for the Puja but His mind was thoroughly engrossed with the love for Sri Vishnu. His dresses were drenched with the tears that fell from His eyes. Getting senses back He left the seat and bathed and wearing another set of fresh dress. Again, the incidence of coming tears happened. Again, He bathed and wore fresh dress but the same state repeated. Mahaprabhu was so possessed in the thoughts (Smaranam) that He could not worship Sri Vishnu with many pujan formalities. At last, Sri Gouranga Mahaprabhu advised His next person and lifelong partner Gadadhar Pundit to sit on the seat and to worship Sri Vishnu with proper formalities.

Seshey Gadadhar prati bolilen vaakya,
Tumi Krishna pujo mor naahika bhaagya.(81)

Mahaprabhu Sri Gourangadev was as Lord Vishnu to the followers and associates. They thought it was better for Gadadhar Pundit to worship Lord Vishnu instead of Mahaprabhu who Himself is Sri Vishnu, Sri Narayana, Sri Krishna.

Mahaprabhu accepted Prasad at Suklambar Brahmachari's house

One day Mahaprabhu remembered that once He took handsful of mixed rice from the begging bag of Suklambar Brahmachari. He called him again and told him that Mahaprabhu would take Prasad at his residence. The poor Suklambar arranged for the Prasad. It was as nice and as rich that even sometime a well to do person cannot afford so much arrangements that Suklambar had arranged. As if Jaganmata Lakshmidevi took the entire responsibility to supply necessary food for Mahaprabhu and His all associates.

There came one Vijaydas and found Lord Sri Krishna at the seat although there was no Deity in the house of Suklambar Brahmachari.

Mahaprabhu went to every house of Nabadwip

Mahaprabhu Sri Gourangadev went to every house of Nabadwip. He met all types of people irrespective of castes, religions and trades. Always Gadadhar, Nityananda, Sribaas, Haridas, Mukunda, Murari, Sridhar, Suklambar, Sanjay and many others remained with Him chanting for Lord Sri Krishna. He personally offered due respect to Conch sellers, Essence sellers, Weavers, Pan sellers, Banana cone and stem seller and many others and all the people gave proper respect to Him. All took Him as own person.

Mahaprabhu's enhanced eagerness for Lord Sri Krishna

Mahaprabhu's eagerness for Kripa of Manjaris, Gopis and of Radharani for having darshan of Lord Sri Krishna enhanced. Mahaprabhu while absorbed in love for Lord Sri Krishna, day after day, now became engaged in search of kindness from the Manjaris and Gopis. Without their Kripa one cannot reach at the feet of Radharani and without Radharani's consent one cannot have darshan of Lord Sri Krishna. The unconditional Love and Service of the Braja Gopis and Radharani had for Lord Sri Krishna that cannot be measured by earthly lives. Seeing Mahaprabhu's searching for Gopis' love for Lord Sri Krishna one of His students, self-styled scholars, one day asked Him –

'Why you utter the names of Gopis? Is not it a wrong thing? Better it was your quest for Sri Krishna only. He took the rein of the chariot of Arjuna. He was a brave hero and a great philosopher rather to say a great politician in that age'.

Mahaprabhu stared at the person but did not like to answer. He wanted to know what the quantity and quality of love for Lord Sri Krishna is. Only Braja Gopis and Vrindavaneswari Radharani know it.

Keha boley sunilaam advuta aakhyan,
Vaishnabey japayey maatra Gopi Gopinaam.(82)

Mahaprabhu Sri Gourangadev wanted to reach more people

Mahaprabhu Sri Gourangadev understood that He should go to more people for propagating the name of Lord Sri Krishna. He should to reach the hearts of millions of people in the Country to unite all for Love to God. He wanted to travel the places in search of love for Lord Sri Krishna. Therefore, He decided to go ahead leaving behind all the attachments had and developed. Nityananda could realize the intention of Mahaprabhu Sri Gouranga.

Nityananda boojhilen Prabhura antar,
Jaanilen Prabhu sighrah chhaariben ghar.(83)

The Effect of Harinaam Movement

Mahaprabhu Sri Gourangadev always remain absorbed in the thoughts of Lord Sri Krishna, Srimati Radha and her Gopis who are engaged in the service for the 'entwined in bliss' the combined souls.

The whole of Nabadwip, the adjacent areas including Shantipur have been flooded with Harinaam Movement. Now Mahaprabhu wants to spread the Movement all over the Country. Therefore, the rest of the places are waiting for His presence and inspiration for joining in the Movement in order to regain the prestige of self-respect and to know own values. Otherwise, man cannot feel the necessity of own work, culture, religion, literature and in every spheres of life. At first man should feel the need of Unity and Integration and man should have a society free of divisions of castes.

Once Mahaprabhu said to others – Chandalohpi Dwijashrestha Haribhakti parayana'. A chandal who lived at the bottom of society is also respectable if he takes Harinaam but if a Brahmin found dishonest should be cursed. He wanted to wipe out all types of differences from the society comprising of different castes, languages, religions, cultures etc. This was His main motto. At almost 24 years of age Mahaprabhu an extraordinary brilliant student and a teacher of high reputation was the only earning and valuable member of the family.

The World awaits Him, decision of Sannyas

Now the time has matured to leave the personal family ties because the whole family of the world awaits

Him. Therefore, He decided to take Sannyas and work for the entire society.

Kshanekey thakur Nityananda hasta dhari,
Nivritey bosilaa giya Gouranga Sri Hari,

Prabhu boley sunah Nityananda mahasaya,
Tomaarey kahiye hridaya nischaya. (84)

Nityananda's reaction on the decision

In reply to Mahaprabhu's intention of taking Sannyas Nityananda understood that Mahaprabhu wants to tear the short tie of family life only in order to serve the Mankind in the World. He is to preach everyone to live with own respect as a Human being. He wants to bring rhythm in daily life of the Mankind. He wants the Unity and Integrity in the society under an umbrella. The Umbrella was to take Harinaam with all. It is mammoth work awaiting a full time Leader. Mahaprabhu is the very Leader suitable from the eastern part of the Country.

Mukunda's reaction on the decision

After getting reply in silence, Mahaprabhu moved to Mukunda's house. Mukunda with his melodious voice sang a song on Lord Sri Krishna. Mahaprabhu then expressed His intention. Mukunda got shocked to know that Mahaprabhu has taken decision of leaving family life for a greater family.

Prabhu boley Mukunda sunaha kichhu katha,
Baahir hoimu aami naa rahibo etha. (85)

Life long partner Pundit Gadadhar's reaction on the decision

Mahaprabhu knew that the people who love Him strongly might not take easily the separation. He informed the life long friend Gadadhar. At first, being so much shocked, Gadadhar Pundit could not speak a single word to Mahaprabhu. He became anxious for what would be the fate of Sachimaa and Vishnupriyadevi? He also felt anxiety that without Mahaprabhu's presence how all the Vaishnavas would survive and continue the movement of Harinaam. All Vaishnavas would die in want of Sri Gouranga as fish die without water. The news seemed to be 'Bold from the Blue' to Gadadhar Pundit.

Mahaprabhu informed only six selected persons

Mahaprabhu informed only six selected persons the decision of Sannyas. They were Nityananda, Mukunda, Gadadhar, Brahmananda, Chandrasekhar and above all Sachimaa. Mahaprabhu strictly cautioned every one of the six not to disclose the decision to anyone else in order to avoid various problems that might arise from various corners. He met all other devotee-friends and spent the day with Samkirtan and discussion on Lord Sri Krishna.

Mother Sachidevi's reaction

Mother Sachidevi cannot resist herself from crying but she was forced to do it lest Vishnupriyadevi knows this and becomes upset. Sachimaa also thought for their neighbourers who could stand on the way of her Nemai. Sachidevi was sure that her Nemai cannot do wrong so she had silent approval for the decision that Nemai had taken. She knew that her Nemai was not only her son but of the whole society. The society needs Him. Mother being a single person should not deprive thousands of the needy men and women of the Country and the whole society. Somehow, she continued her domestic work.

Sridhar presented a bottle-gourd, someone brought some milk. Sachidevi boiled the pieces of gourd in the milk. Mahaprabhu after taking food went to bed.

Gadadhar Pundit and Haridas

Haridas came and remained with Gadadhar at the doorstep of Mahaprabhu's bedroom.

Nikatey suilaa Haridas Gadadhar. (86)

Mahaprabhu left home forever

Very early in the morning before the crows step on the earth from the branches of their dwelling trees Mahaprabhu got ready to set for. Gadadhar and Haridas woke up. They insisted Mahaprabhu to take them with Him.

Gadadhar Haridas uthilen jaani,
Gadadhar bolen chaliba sangey aami. (87)

Sri Gouranga Mahaprabhu said no to them. He set for Katwa alone advising them to meet next day at Katwa.

At first He worshipped towards mother Sachidevi saying- Mother, my dear mother, you have done for me lot. This body is your award to me. I never could serve for you. I just received your affection and results of your good qualities. I know I shall not be able to repay your debt in lives after lives. I shall remain indebted to you for ever. I know in the mortal world we come here for a few days and after some time we go back to Him. So please do not mind. Before it happens I am going for Sannyas. Please mother, do not mind. I assure, you will have no problem mother. Lord Sri Krishna will look after you all the time. Take it granted as the wishes of God Lord Sri Krishna.

Dear mother please allow me to go. Do not get worried for me. Good bye Mother, good bye –

> Jananira padadhuli loi Prabhu shirey,
> Pradakshin kori taarey chalilaa sattwarey,
>
> Chalilen Boikuntha nayak griha hoitey,
> Sannyas koriya sov jiv uddhaaritey. (88)"

Sri Gouranga Mahaprabhu walked much before dawn and reached the Ghat on the bank of the Ganga. The Ghat later, was named as *Nidaya Ghat* (i.e. without kindness).Mahaprabhu crossed the Ganga by swimming.

11

The Sannyas

Mahaprabhu Sri Gourangadev at Katwa

At last, He reached Katwa. As he advised the associates like Sri Nityananda, Sri Gadadhar, Sri Haridas, Mukunda, Chandrasekhar and Brahmananda came over there.

Sri Abadhuta Chandra Gadadhar Mukunda,

Sri Chandrasekhar Acharya aar Brahmananda. (89)

Mahaprabhu wiped out His identity as Brahmin at First

Then Keshab Bharati reached the place. Other people, devotees or non-devotees, assembled around Mahaprabhu. The barber Madhu sat to abolish the tuft that indicates a symbol of a Brahmin first then to shave the beautiful hair of Sri Gouranga Mahaprabhu.

Keshav Bharati, the Preceptor with Others

The people having heard the news of Mahaprabhu's decision gathered around Sri Gourangadev and other associates. They were stunned to see that such a young and nice looking strong and stout young man is taking Sannyas. They, including the barber Madhuand the associates started to cry loudly. However, Gourangadev is Gourangadev. With tears in his eyes the barber abolished the tuft the symbol of Brahminism. Keshav Bharati also shed tears to see a gentle man of only 24 years' youth is taking Sannyas from him.

The Initiation for Sannyas and Sri Krishnachaitanya

Gouranga Mahaprabhu wanted to abolish caste system that prevailed for a long years and made the society crippled. He did not prefer any differences in human beings. After totally shaved the hair Gouranga Mahaprabhu with tears in eyes for Love of Lord Shri Krishna sat before Keshav Bharati and he awarded initiation for asceticism. Bharati did not consider to award his surname 'Bharati' in the line established by Jagadguru Shankaracharya. Keshab Bharati awarded Sri Gouranga the name as **Sri Krishnachaitanya**, the conscient personality and the person who made others conscious about Lord Sri Krishna. Keshab Bharati also said to Mahaprabhu – You are God Yourself'. It was a justified name for Him.

The date was 1431 Saka 916 Bengali Sal 2nd Magha (possibly 18 Feb. 1510 A.D.). (90)

All present there started to chant Harinaam with much more enthusiasm encircling Sri Chaitanyadev.

Bhaktagan mukha heri nachayey aanandey,
Aapaney thakur naachey – Nityanandey,

Gadadhar Narahari naachey – kaachhe kaachhey,
Sakal Vaishnav naachey – Gourahari maajhey. (91)

Mahaprabhu Sri Chaitanyadev moved west for Mahura-Vrindavan

Nextday Mahaprabhu Sri Chaitanyadev started to move towards the west in order to go to Mahura-Vrindavan where Lord Sri Krishna did His Divine exposed Lila. Sri Chaitanyadev knew very well that God's Divine Lila is eternal and it is happening in the Universe. No one can deny that there remains the importance of memory of Lord Sri Krisha in Mathura – Vrindavan – Dwarka like places. All the associates including Keshab Bharati started to follow Him. By running speedily through the Rarh areas full with flowers like Shimul and Palash and the sweet breeze at the entrance of the Spring. Wherever Mahaprabhu went He sang and danced for Lord Sri Krishna. On the way at some villages, many people came out to see the Sannyasi and others who always preferred to chant the Harinaam. Most of them were surprised to note the Divine look of a young person Mahaprabhu as Sannyasi and always in deep sense of Lord Sri Krishna.

A boy shoutedly uttered the Harinaam

However, at some villages Mahaprabhu noted that none is interested to utter the name of God. It disheartened Mahaprabhu. Once He thought that it is better to jump into the water in any pond as none takes Harinaam. His associates tried to console Him. At last, a boy from a grazing ground shoutedly uttered the

Harinaam. Mahaprabhu greeted the boy by patting on his back.

Kenduli village Poet Jaydev of Geeta Govinda

We can remember the place Kenduli just on the bank of the Ajoy river in the district of Birbhum. It is believed that once Poet Jayadev, a poet of the court of Raja Lakshman Sen, lived at Kenduli village. Jaydev, the writer of the Geetagovinda, was also a regular worshipper of Kusheswar Shiva. Mahaprabhu went towards the west upto eight miles away from Bakreswar. From there, He returned towards the east to find the way to Neelachal.

Mahaprabhu arrived back at the bank of the Ganga

Mahaprabhu reached near the bank of the Ganga opposite side of Shantipur and bathed in the water of the Ganga considering the river as Ymuna, where on the bank in the Divine forest Vrindavan Lord Sri Krishna played the eternal Lila. He recited sloka for Yamuna –

"Chidanandabhaanoh Sadananda Sunoh
Parama Prempatri Drabat Brahmagatri

Aghanang Labitri Jagatkshemdhatri Pabitri
Kriyanno Rapurmitraputri". (92)

At Fulia

Sri Chaitanyadev went to Fulia, the village of Haridas and sent Nityananda towards Nabadwip advising him to tell all others that He would go to Puri after staying a few days at Adwaitacharya's house at Shantipur. At Fulia thousands of people of different castes including all kinds of physically handicapped persons rushed to Him. All saw Mahaprabhu Sri Chaitanyadev with tears in His eyes for love of Lord Sri Krishna and all were beloved by Mahaprabhu.

Nityananda at Nabadwip and found Sachimaa fasting

On the other hand, Nityananda reached Nabadwip and found Sachimaa was fasting for twelve days in the shock of son's departure. The same condition as a mad was for Vishnupriya Devi. He consoled both the mother and the wife of Sri Chaitanyadev and somehow managed Sachimaa to break the fasting by taking Prasad otherwise the worshipped God would remain without regular Bhog. He also informed all the details to Sribaas and other devotees.

Subhavaani Nityananda kahen sabaarey,
Sattar chalaha sovey Prabhu dekhibarey,

Shantipur gelaa Prabhu Acharyera gharey,
Aami aailaam toma sabaarey nibaarey. . - Nityananda advised all the associates to meet Mahaprabhu at the residence of Adwaitacharya at Shantipur. (93)

Sri Chaitanyadev at Adwaitacharya's house at Shantipur

Mahaprabhu Sri Chaitanyadev arrived at Adwaitacharya's house at Shantipur. He found at first Adwaitacharya's child nakedly was playing on dust. Mahaprabhu took the child in His arms effectiontely. He told the child Achyutananda – I also regard Adwaitacharya as my father and then we are brothers'.

Nityananda arrived at Shantipur accompanying Sachimaa in a Palanquin. Mother seeing her son's shaved head cried a lot. Other hundreds devotees who arrived there from Nabadwip also cried loudly. Mahaprabhu Sri Chaitanyadev seeing mother at first bowed His head by touching all the limbs on ground.

Sachimaa at Adwaitacharya's house and cooked delicious items for her son

Then seeing other devotees from Nabadwip Mahaprabhu became overwhelmed. All started to chant Harinaam encircling Mahaprabhu. It continued for a long time. Sachimaa inside Adwaitacharya's house prepared delicious items as Mahaprabhu preferred.

Yabat Acharya grihey Nemair abasthaan,
Mui viksha dimoo sovaarey ei mango daan.(94)

Adwaitacharya's house became full of Joy

Adwaitacharya's house remained joyful for ten days. Sachidevi although aspired that Mahaprabhu should remain nearer but Sri Chaitanyadev convinced her and she was pleased to know that her Nemai would generally remain at Neelachal and would be able to come back at Shantipur off and on. Moreover, other devotees may also bring His information from Puri at regular intervals.

12

Sri Chaitanyadev on Way to Neelachal

Critical Situation of Travelling

The time was passing in critical situation. Mahaprabh Sri Chaitanyadev cared little. All the devotees ran after Mahaprabhu. Taking a pause, Mahaprabhu said to all to return to own places. He advised everyone to become a sincere as familyman and to chant Harinaam and always to discuss topics on Sri Krishna. However, six of the associates did not leave Him alone.

Mahaprabhu Chaitanyadev now is on the way of Neelachal i.e. Puri where the Temple of Lord Jagannath is gloriously situated. The associates like Nityananda, Gadadhar, Mukunda, Gobinda, Jagadnanda and Brahmananda accompanied and walked through the district of 24 Parganas by the eastern bank of the Ganga.

At Chhatrabhog

They reached Chhatrabhog in the southern part of 24 Parganas, a place of Shiva. Under the water there is established Shiva as Ambulinga. Mahaprabhu gave hearty respect to Ambulinga and made all the people there happy by performing Kirtan and dances with all the devotees present.

Ramchandra Khan

Here a devotee Ramchandra Khan a trustworthy and well to do zeminder and a Subedar, representative of Hussain Shah. His area of zeminderi was much bigger. Once somehow, Ramchandra Khan failed to pay the taxes due and therefore he got temporary imprisonment into the jail of the ruler. His relatives collected huge amount of money in order to to pay up dues for his early release. Ramchandra Khan understood that the amount so accumulated would not be sufficient for releasing a zeminder of big areas like him. He advised to deposit the whole amount in the treasury in favour of other captive zeminders of smaller areas and whose dues were lesser. Within a few days, many small zeminders got released at a time as their dues have been paid up. This incident drew the attention of Hussain Shah and he was surprised to note the benevolence Ramchandra Khan had shown for others. Hussain Shah waived all the dues of Ramchandra and awarded him with a title Mahasay (Sir, Khan). Since then, his power and influence enhanced.

There at Chhatrabhog, Sri Chaitanyadev with the associates and the villagers engaged in Samkirtan. All danced and sang the songs for Lord Sri Krishna. Ramchandra Khan arranged a boat for Sri Chaitanyadev and the accompanying devotees to reach Orissa.

On boat all sang and danced for Lord Sri Krishna

All of the devotees including Sri Chaitanya Mahaprabhu started to sing and dance on the boat. The boat was about to sink and so the sailor requested them not to sing loudly lest their sound could reach the ears of dacoits and if they come they shall not spare them but to loot all their belongings and kill all by throwing into the water. At that time, the political and administrative situation on both sides of Bengal and Orissa were much critical and tensified. There was nobody to care and to look after the safety of passers-by in the borders.

At Prayag ghat, Temple of Shiva Mahesh

However, Mahaprabhu with others reached at Prayag Ghat in Utkal. He took bath in the ghat and worshipped in Temple of Shiva Mahesh. People there believe that Yudhisthira of the Mahabharata erected the Temple. All people there greeted Mahaprabhu and offered many things so that He could arrange food for all His associates. Jagadananda cooked food for all. In the Shiva Temple area all stayed and covered the whole night by chanting the Harinaam.

Whether such Quantity of Tears a Human Body can Contain

At the border of Bengal-Orissa, an entry tax collector demanded necessary taxes from all. He seeing a mendicant excused Mahaprabhu and asked all the people whether they belong to Him but Mahaprabhu's reply in ambiguity could not satisfy him. Therefore, the collector did not allow others to cross the line. Having crossed the border Mahaprabhu Sri Chaitanyadev sat under a tree and started to chant in love of Lord Sri Krishna. His eyes were full of tears. Tears were coming from inside and drenched the place. The collector, again being requested by Mahaprabhu's associates, came to Him to take clear confirmation that the people are of His own but was surprised to note that Mahaprabhu crying for Lord Sri Krishna and huge amount of tears were coming out. He could not understand whether a human body can contain such amount of tears. Thus being satisfied he allowed all and with folded hands begged mercy from Sri Chaitanya Mahaprabhu.

Dani boley e purush narah kobhu nahey,
Manushyer nayaney ki eta dhara bohey. (95)

Sri Niyananda broke the Stick of Mahaprabhu

Jagadananda was carrying Mahaprabhu's Stick a sign of Sannyasi. At the bank of the river Subarnarekha Mahaprabhu waited for all for sometime and left the place before Jagadananda and Nityananda Prabhu arrived. Jagadananda felt the time for begging kept the Stick of Mahaprabhu to Nityananda. Nityananda engrossed with the love for Lord Sri Krishna and Sri Chaitanya Mahaprabhu became almost restless. To see the Stick in his hand he laughingly thought – I am sufficient to bear Mahaprabhu, this Stick has no use more". Therefore, he broke the Stick.

Auhey danda aami jaarey bahiyey hridayaey,
Se tomaarey bohiben eto jukta nahey,

Eta boli Balaram parama prachanda,
Phelilen danda bhaangi kori tin khanda. (96)

Jagadananda showed the broken pieces of the Stick. Mahaprabhu said that the Stick also contain God in it. Then Mahaprabhu added that only an earthly material was in His possession and now that has been damaged.

Let it be now. He is more free from anything of earthly materials.

At Jaleswar

Mahaprabhu arrived at Jaleswar and there He sang and danced with the drums and other musical instruments active in full swing there in love for God. All people were surprised to find a Vaishnav having such devotion in a Shiva Temple. Then Mahaprabhu embraced all and advised also to offer due respect to Nityananda.

Sabarey sikhaya Gour Chandra Bhagawan,
Nityananda prati savey hao saabdhaan,

Mor deha hoitey Nityananda deha bado,
Satya satya sabaarey kohinu ei darah. (97)

At Bansdhaya met certain Shakti devotee

Near Bansdhaya, they all met with a devotee of Shakti. Mahaprabhu talked to him friendly and took information of other sincere Shakti devotees. He gladly accepted the invitation to be present at their Temple.

Khirchora Gopinath Deity at Remuna

From Bansdhaya Mahaprabhu arrived at Remuna where the Temple of Khirchora Gopinath is situated. It is heard, that once the Deity himself had stolen one pot of Khir (delicious condensed sweet made of milk) from the twelve pots. Gopinath Himself has stolen one pot and kept behind His wrapper and as a boy went to Madhabendra Puri and offered the khir bhog to the hungry devotees Madhabendra Puri and his disciple Iswarpuri. It is also in belief that in dream Gopinath advised the priest of the Temple to find the stolen khir from His behind and to hand it over to Madhabendra puri.

Since then, the Deity of Gopinath was named as Khirchora Gopinath. To see the Gopinath Deity and remembering the name of Madhabendra Puri Mahaprabhu Chaitanyadev sang songs and danced with all the associates and lost His senses with love for Lord Sri Krishna.

Remunate Gopinath Parama Mohan,
Bhakti kori koila Prabhu Tnaar Darashan. (98)

Sri Chaitanyadev at every Shiva Temple

Mahprabhu Sri Chaitanyadev bowed at every Shiva Temple and there He chanted the songs on Lord Sri Krishna and recited Shiva Pranam. We can remember that Sri Nityananda was also a worshipper of Lord Shiva at Ekchakra village in the district of Birbhum and as a Abadhoot he used to carry a small blue Linga stone as Shiva in a bag hanging from his neck.

At Jajpur the place of Temples

Sri Chaitanyadev then arrived at Jajpur in Orissa. There were innumerable Temples of many Deities of gods and goddesses at Jajpur. Alone Mahaprabhu roamed almost the whole day the places and everywhere sang and danced in love for Lord Sri Krishna.

At Cuttack, Sakshi Gopal

After having holy bath in the Mahanadi, He reached Cuttack. There, Mahaprabhu visited the Temple where the Deity of Sakshigopal remains. It is believed that Lord Sri Krishna from Vrindaban came Himself on foot in order to register His witness for favour of one of His devotees. The episode prevailing for long back, that one senior Brahmin on his pilgrimage became seriously ill and was left behind by tne villagers and relatives for die. Only one accompanying Brahmin boy bravely stayed, nursed and cured him. After complete healing the senior person being satisfied gave assurance to his junior company to get him married with his daughter. There was none to listen the words of assurances but the Deity of Gopal was in the Temple. Therefore, the Deity of Gopal was regarded only as witness. It is believed that Deity of Gopal started to move with the Brahmin boy on his way to return home but cautioned not to look behind. The Brahmin boy crossed miles after miles but did not look back for a while. They entered Orissa and the boy was almost nearer to his residence and for a while he wanted to be sure whether the black stone Deity was really coming and still walking along with him for standing as a witness on his favour. Alas, the Deity stopped the journey and stood there as a stone made Deity of Gopal - Lord Sri Krishna only.

Gopal soundarya dekhi lokey anandita,
'Pratima chali aaila' suni hoila bishmita,

Tobey sei bada bipra anandita hoiyan,
Gopaaler aagete pade dandabot hoiyan,

Sakal lokera aagey Gopal saakshi dila,
Bada bipra chhoto biprey kanyadaan dila. (99)

Mahprabhu Sri Chaitanyadev recollected the episode and cried in love of God.

At Bhubaneswar and Kamalpur

After visiting the Shiva Temple in Bhubaneswar Mahaprabhu reached Kamalpur and from distance found the top of the Jagannath Temple. Mahaprabhu became almost mad to find the top of the Temple where Lord Sri Krishna remains as Jagannath, with Balaram and Subhadra.

Arrived at the Holy Temple of Lord Jagananth, Balaram and Subhadra

With uttering, the name of Lord Sri Krishna Mahaprabhu ran towards the Temple alone and reached there. He wanted to touch the Deity of Lord Jagannath in order to embrace Lord but the guards denied to allow Him to do it in the Temple. Mahaprabhu fainted and fell on the floor in love for God. The guards were about to beat Mahaprabhu. Fortunately, Sarbabhoum Bhattacharya an influential pundit, trusted personality of the King of Orissa was present there, and he somehow saved the life and arranged to carry the fainted body of Lord Sri Chaitanya to his house. Nityananda, Gadadhar, Mukunda, Jagadananda, Gobinda, Brahmananda and other devotees came, knew the situation, bowed at the main entrance of the Temple and rushed to the house of Sarbabhoum where Mahaprabhu got shelter for the time being.

13

Mahaprabhu in Neelachal and Southern India Travel

At Sarbabhoum's house

Getting normal senses Mahaprabhu found Sarbabhoum and all the associates who came from Shantipur with Him. He promised to them from this day He would see Lord Jagannath from the Pillar only.

Mahaprabhu Sri Chaitanyadev and Sarbabhoumacharya

Sarbabhoum Bhattacharya was senior to Mahaprabhu in age. He, earlier, learnt the Nayashastra (Logic) in Mithila. At the time of return home in Bengal he was forbidden to carry any book or paper with him. Before the appearance of Lord Gouranga, Sarbabhoum with his talent and extra ordinary memory opened a school of Nayashastra, thus with the efforts of Sarbabhoum and afterwards Raghunath Siromani, Jagadish Pundit, Gadadhar Pundit and others the place Nabadwip became an important centre of learning Nayashastra. He was regarded as one of the the prime Pundits of the whole Country and abroad. Therefore, he wanted to offer some ideas on Adyaitbad to this young and talented Sannyasi Sri Chaitanyadev. Sri Chaitanyadev has shown immense patience in the class during a period of seven days. He did not speak a single word. To see Sri Chaitanya's silence throughout the classes Sarbabhoum assumed all the topics he taught in the classes were not apprehensible by younger Sri Chaitanyadev. So he asked Him the reason, if any, was behind this. Sri Chaitanyadev very humbly answered that He did not prefer the narration without devotion to Lord Sri Krishna. Sarbabhoum became stunned and ultimately by leaving behind the way of Logic and teachings of Vedanta, he dived into the world of devotion. He felt Chaitanyadev as the Puranpurush Lord Vishnu. He saw the six-handed Lord Sri Krishna and understood that Lord Sri Krishna Himself has appeared on this world to preach Bhakti the devotion towards God. He started to consider Sri Chaitanyadev as Lord Sri Krishna Himself. It is heard, later, although Mahaprabhu had forbidden to tell others, he himself drawn a sketch of six handed Sri Chaitanyadev in the Temple of Lord Jagannath.

Sarbabhoum and Others in Puri joined in the Harinaam Movement

The news of participation of a renowned scholar like Sarbabhoum in the Harinaam Movement with Sri Chaitanyadev with invisible wings reached the corners of the Country. The people of Orissa from villages and towns came to Puri to see Lord Sri Chaitanyadev's hearty devotion for Lord Sri Krishna with tears in His eyes and Harinaam in His lips swinging all the time. Many of them joined the team of Samkirtan. Among them Pradyumna Mishra, Premanada, Ramananda, Damodar Pundit, Srisankar, Pradyumna Brahmachari, Bhagaban Acharya became associates of Lord Sri Chaitanyadev. Thus within a short period of time the pilgrimage Puri became full of Samkirtan with songs on Lord Sri Krishna by Sri Chaitanyadev and His associates of Bengal and Orissa. Mahaprabhu on the seashore spent the evening time with chanting Harinaam with others. Mahaprabhu preferred to listen the Bhagawat from His lifelong partner Gadadhar Pundit.

A Well at Paramananda Puri's Ashram

One day He went to Paramananda Puri's Ashram and found a well with dirty smelled water. Mahaprabhu prayed to the Ganga and ashtonishingly clear water flowed in the well. Mahaprabhu spent two months in Puri including His participation in the Dolyatra Festival there.

Mahaprabhu travelled Southern part in India

Mahaprabhu decided to travel in the whole of South India and possibly, the month of Baisakh after 15th April 1510 A.D. started His journey. Then paths on His way were not smooth or metalled. These were narrow, rough and through forests, bushes, hills and many rivers big or small. Sri Chaitanyadev decided to trek alone towards the South. He travelled the whole of Southern part in India for long two years alone on bare feet.

Krishnadas went to assist Mahaprabhu

At last all decided to send a man named Krishnadas for Mahaprabhu to assist Him for holding the minimum belongings. Krishnadas accompanied Mahaprabhu in order to carry the water pot and wares for Mahaprabhu's use.

All upto Alalnath

However, all including Sri Gadadhar Pundit, Sri Nityananda accompanied with Mahaprabhu Sri Chaitanyadev unto Alalnath and from there, Mahaprabhu started to walk alone towards the South.

Gadadhar Pundit remained in Puri

Gadadhar Pundit His constant company from Childhood has to remain in Puri with Kshetra Sannyas being engaged to worship Tota Gopinath, the Deity that Mahaprabhu revealed from beneath the sands of the sea beach of Puri.

Yatra for South India

Mahaprabhu walked miles after miles on bare feet through forests, hills, narrow paths, crossed rivers, tolerated rains, storms, cold and schorching sunrays. Notihng could hinder Him from moving one place to another with songs in lips-

'Haraey namah Krishna Jadavaya namah

Gopala Govinda Ramah Sri Madhusudana

Or

Krishna Krishna Krishna Krishna Krishna Krishna Krishnahey.

Krishna Krishna Krishna Krishna Krishna Krishna Krishnahey.

Krishna Krishna Krishna Krishna Krishna Krishna Rakshamum.

Krishna Krishna Krishna Krishna Krishna Krishna Paahimum.

Rama Raghava Rama Raghava Rama Raghava Rakshamum.

Krishna Keshava Krishna Keshava Krishna Keshava Paahimum.

Krishnadas just tried to follow Mahaprabhu or His sounds of songs. In South India Mahaprabhu traveled - Alalnath, Simhachalam and the River Godavari, Vidyanagar, Koti Lingeswar Shiva temple, Markendaya temple, Draksharam, Palkannu, Vimabharam, and a Shiva temple at Antarvedi, passing Vijayawada and the river the Krishnaa, Mahaprabhu arrived at Mangalgiri on the lap of East Coast Mountains. There remains the Deity of Nrisinghadeva, and also Rajalakshmi, Shrisailam, Abaloham, Siddhoibat, Trijuni, Sri Kaalhasti-Briddha Kasi, Thirupati-Thirumalai, Kanchipuram, Shivakanchi, Mahabalipuram, Chidambaram, Kumbhakonam, Srirangam, Trichinapalli, Sri Shaila, Durbeshan, Mahendra hill, Tamraparni in Pandyasthan, Kanyakumari,Vellimalai,Thiruvattura, Thiruvanthapuram: Pediar-Payashwini, Guruvaur-Calicut-Shringeri, Udipi, Bellur Tritakupa, Jog Falls-Panchapsara, Gokarna, Pottakadal, Mahabaleswar. It is also said by some writers that Sri Chaitanyadev visited Pune, the centre of education from ancient times then Khandabat, Daman, Surat, Broch, Baroda and Dakor and again Baroda, Ahmedabad and crossed the river Sabarmoti or Subhramoti to reach Dwarka and on His way Somnath Temple. Then by the sides of the river the Narmada and the Godavari by passing through Dohad, Mandalnagar, Devghar, Shibaninagar, Malaya hills,

Chandipur and Raipur. He visited some other places. He started to return. He received immense love and recognition from the places where He sang and danced in Love for Lord Sri Krishna. He had immense love for the People all everywhere.

In the tour He with Roy Ramananda established the Sadhya Sadhan Tattwa on the bank of the Godavari. He also at Srirangam discovered Gopal Bhatta who later took part in editing the Haribhaktivilas in collaboration with Sri Sanatan in Vrindavan. He discovered Brahma Samhita and Krishnakarnamrita and copied them.

Mahaprabhu Sri Chaitanyadev and Roy Ramananda

Earlier, at the beginning of trekking Mahaprabhu Sri Chaitanyadev bathed in the river Godavari and sang the songs of Lord Sri Krishna and on the other hand, Roy Ramananda with his royal team reached the ghat of the Godavari for taking his daily bath. Both of them recognized each other. They discussed the love of God and the love for God. There they in ten days' discussion established the Sadhya Sadhan Tatwa an important philosophy of Goudiya Vaishnavism. Thousands of people of different ideologies were attracted to His sweet Kirtan and gathered around Him while He madly sang and danced in the name of Lord Sri Krishna. Many people converted themselves into the belief of Vaishnavism.

Chhaya Sita Murti

When Mahaprabhu went to Dakshin Mathura there lived Ramdas a devotee of Sri Ramchandra and Mahaprabhu accepted his invitation for alms. But surprisingly He noticed that Ramdas only thinking of Lord

Sri Ramchandra during all the time and made no arrangement of cooking for himself or Sri Mahaprabhu till the midday. He asked the reason. Ramdas replied that Lakshman has gone into the deep forest to collect fruits and other vegetables and after return Sita mother would cook. But, alas the *rakshas* king Ravana has taken away mother Sitadevi. Rakshas (devil) has touched the holy mother Sitadevi and so living by taking food has no meaning to him. It was an impossible matter to make understand such a devotee of Sri Ram, however Sri Chaitanyadev told him: -

Sitadevi is loved by Lord and Herself is the Chidanada and with earthly eyes we cannot see Her. She is beyond to touch and She is ever with us. Ravana could only take the shadow Sita away. The devotee should not repent and he should take prasada daily to live in this world to worship Lord Ramchandra otherwise he would die in starvation.

"Ishwarpreyasi Sita Chidananda Murti,

Prakrita Indriye Taren Dekhite Nari.

and He said again,

Aprakrita Bastu Nahe Prakrita Gochar,

Veda Puranete ei Kahe Nirantar." (2)

Ramdas started to consider Sri Chaitanyadev as his Sri Ramchandra. He was delighted much.

After taking bath at Kritamalay Mahaprabhu went to Durbeshan and visited the temple of Raghunathji i.e. Sri Ramchandra.

At Mahendra hill He paid respect to Parshuram. He went to Setubandha and bathed at Dhonu Pilgrim and in Ramaswar visited the Temple and decided to take a pause for listening the Kurma Purana that supported His saying what He consoled Ramdas at south Mathura earlier. He copied the explanation portion Himself and again retuned to Dakshin Mathura to show Ramdas the devotee of Sri Ramchandra :-

Sitayaradhito banhichchhaya Sitamaji janat.

Twang jahara dasha gribah Sita banhipurah gata.

Pariksha samaye banhing chhaya Sita bibasa saa.

Banhi Sitang samaniya tatpurus tadaneenayat.

Nabadha Bhakti

Thereafter arrived at the temple of Bal Gopal established by Madhyacharya. Here also Mahaprabhu had to establish Bhaktidharma the religion of Love and Devotion after some debates with local worshippers.

He sang from Srimadbhagawata –

"Shravanang Kirtanang Vishnoh Smaranang Paadasevanam

Archanang Vandanang Dasyang Sakshyamatmanivedanam.

That expresses (as Prahlad suggested father Hiranyakashipu) that if a devotee who considers worshipping the Lord Sri Krishna he should have any of the nine qualities : of Listening, Singing for God, Remembering, Serving at the Feet of Lord, Worshipping, Praising, becoming a Servant, Friendly and Surrendering everything even oneself completely to Him is the best way of pleasing Lord Sri Krishna and that is the best lessons learning.

It is also said by some writers that Sri Chaitanyadev visited Pune, the centre of education from ancient times then Khandabat, Daman, Surat, Broch, Baroda and Dakor and again Baroda, Ahmedabad and crossed the river Sabarmoti or Subhramoti to reach Dwarka and on His way Somnath Temple. The by the sides of the river the Narmada and the Godavari by passing through Dohad, Mandalnagar, Devghar, Shibaninagar, Malaya hills, Chandipur, Raipur and some other places. He started to return. He received immense love and recognition from the places where He sang and danced in Love for Lord Sri Krishna. He had immense love for the People all everywhere.

At last after two years' vigorious journey on foot only Sri Chaitanya Mahaprabhu returned at Vidyanagar the place of Roy Ramananda. Roy Ramananda with some waiting devotees rushed to Him and both embraced each other. Sri Chaitanya Mahaprabhu read the two unavailable scriptures *Brahmasamhita* and *Krishnakarnamritam* to Roy Ramananda who arranged to copy the Scriptures.

Returned to Neelachal

After seven days' stay at Vidyanagar with Roy Ramananda Sri Chaitanya Mahaprabhu decided to return to Neelachal where the Deity of Lord Jagannath remains with Balaram and Subhadra in the Temple. Pundit Gadadhar, Nityananda, Jagananda, Damodar Pundit, Mukunda, Gopinath Acharya and other devotees all came to receive Him. Sarbabhoum Bhattacharya also reached the Sea-shore to receive Him cordially and they embraced each other. Krishnadas having been released from duty rushed to Nabadwip to meet mother Sachidevi and to give her the information that after completing tour in the South Sri Chaitanyadev has returned to Puri, Neelachal.

Neelachal the place of Lord Jagannath is in the heart of people of Orissa and Bengal and of all the states of India for pilgrimage and also for the beautiful Sea Beach, now the place has got an additional attraction for Lord Sri Chaitanyadev. He sang and danced glorifying Lord Sri Krishna i.e. Lord Jagannath there.

His Residence at Kashi Mishra's House

Sarbabhoum Acharya having discussion with the Raja Pratp Rudra made an arrangement of His residence at Kashi Mishra's house. Kashi Mishra visualised the four handed Sri Krishna in Mahaprabhu Sri Chaitanyadev. Devotees from Goud Bengal and of Utkal all assembled in the house. More devotees from Utkal like Janardan, Shikhi Mahity, Murari Mahity, Murari Mishra, Vishnudas, Praharaj Mahapatra, Paramananda Mahapatra and Roy Ramananda's father Bhabananda Roy with son Baninath for rendering service to Sri Chaitanyadev.

Another Prominent Baninath

Another prominent Baninath an associate of Sri Chaitanyadev was son of Madhab Mishra and brother of

Gadadhar Pundit. This Baninath had two sons, one them was poet and composer of devotional songs Sri Nayanananda and the other was Sri Hridayananda. Unmarried Gadadhar Pundit arranged proper education and brought up the latter. One of Mahaprabhu's associates Gouridas Pundit of Ambika Kalna begged him from Gadadhar Pundit. At Kalna Hridayananda kept Mahaprabhu's Deity in his heart. (100)

Swaroop Damodar

In order to join with Mahaprabhu Sri Chaitanyadev there at Kashi Mishra's house Gambhira arrived Swaroop Damodar. During the Nabadwip Lila Damodar, known as Purushottam Pundit was also an active person. Knowing Mahaprabhu's Sannyas he also considered not to reside in Nabadwip without Sri Gouranga Mahaprabhu. He leaving Nabadwip went in Varanasi and got Sannyas initiation from Chaitanyananda. With preceptor's direction he started teachings on Vedanta. He was a remarkable scholar and a singer of high quality. After taking initiation of Sannyas mantra, he did not leave his sacred thread and tuft. He did not accept the title like Giri, Puri etc. He remained same as himself. Therefore, he was in his *Swaroop* and known as Swaroop Damodar. He, after taking Preceptor's consent, came to Neelachal and took the responsibility of looking after all *sevas* of Mahaprabhu and once became the second man to Mahaprabhu in Gambhira. He, in addition, took the task of examining anything written by anybody and given to Mahaprabhu for His reading.

Bhakti siddhanta viruddha yei, aar rasabhas,
Sunitey naa hoi Prabhur chitter ullhaas. (101).

14

In Goud Banga and Mathura Vrindavan

Mahaprabhu Started for Goud Banga

After a few months of South India travel, Mahaprabhu decided to come back Bengal for having a bath in the water of the river Ganga and to see Mother Sachimaa and also to visit some places. Thousands of devotees and ordinary people of Goud Bengal were eagerly awaiting the safe return of Sri Chaitanya Mahaprabhu from the vast South India.

Gadadhar Pundit Desired to Accompany

The accompanying team comprised of Ramananda Paramananda Puri, Swaroop Damodar, Jagadananda, Gobinda, Bakreswar, Mukunda and other followers. Here Sri Chaitanyadev did not take His life long associate Gadadhar Pundit but Gadadhar himself started to walk with loving friend Sri Chaitanyadev because it was a prior decision that after visiting Goud Bengal and the river Ganga Sri Chaitanyadev would go to Mathura-Vrindavan alone. Gadadhar cannot let Sri Chaitanyadev go alone to Mathura-Vrindavan. Earlier Gadadhar allowed Sri Chaitanyadev for South India tour for a long period of two years and now it would be difficult for him to live for a single day without seeing and serving Sri Chaitanya Mahaprabhu.

Sri Chaitanyadev wanted to convince him to stay in Puri with the worshipping of Tota Gopinath, the Deity recovered from under the sand of the sea beach. He tried to console Gadadhar that to serve Tota Gopinath will be sufficient as he used to and liked to serve Mahaprabhu. But, Gadadhar Pundit was like an unyielding child and at last he said – O.k., I'm going alone to see Sachimaa in Goud Bengal. I shall choose a separate path'.

Mahaprabhu Sri Chaitanyadev could not speak a single word against this topic as He Himself was feeling thirst to see the Mother, the Motherland and the Mother river Ganga. He was full of anxiety for lone traveller Gadadhar and the worshipping of Tota Gopinath. From way at Cuttack He called for Gadadhar Pundit back and told him- I understand your extreme happiness to be with me but it would be a cause of my sorrow if you give up your duty for some days also. I hope you do not want to see me in a condition of sorrow for you. If you want my pleasure please go back Neelachal.'

Mahaprabhu in Goud Banga

Sri Chaitanyadev returned Bengal after crossing Panihati, Kumarhatta (Halisahar), Kanchanpalli (Kanchrapara) and then decided to stay at Vidyanagar where Vidyabachaspati's one son of Maheswar Visharad resides. We can remember another son of Visharad was

Sarbabhoum of Neelachal. There Mahaprbhu took bath in the water of the river Ganga and wanted to stay only by chanting the name of Lord Sri Krishna lonely for a few days and thereafter He could start journey for Vrindavan-Mathura.

Millions of People Assembled to have Darshan of Mahaprabhu

However the news of His stay there was spread all over Bengal within a short period and thousands of people from different corners started to flock together there to have a glimpse of Lord Sri Chaitanyadev. Some came also by swimming in the river Ganga as all the boats were overloaded each time while crossed the river. Mahaprabhu preferred a solitary place to take rest and chant the name of Lord Sri Krishna before expected journey. To see the unthinkable and uncontrollable crowd accumulated everyday one fine morning with some of His followers Mahaprabhu went to Kuliya at the house of Madhabdas Chattopadhyay. The assembled people did not believe it and thought that it is nothing but a trick of Vidyabachaspati to have the scope of serving Sri Chaitanyadev alone and so he has kept hidden Sri Chaitanyadev inside the house. They shouted and repeatedly requested him to arrange at least one appearance of Sri Chaitanyadev to quench the thirst of the eyes of the people.

Within a few days, knowing the truth Vidyabachaspati with all the people rushed to Kuliya to have a darshan of Lord Sri Chaitanyadev.

Mahaprabhu forgave Gopal Chapal and met Others

Here Mahaprabhu forgave Gopal Chapal, met Bakreswar Pundit, tantrik Krishnananda and many followers. There came Devananda Pundit who used to read and teach the Srimad Bhagabata to listeners and students. Mahaprabhu explained to him that without devotion *(BHAKTI)* the Bhagawata should not be read out to everyone. The eternal love cannot be discussed everywhere to any person without Bhakti. Both the reader and the listeners should be mentally prepared to have the eternal Rasa Sri Krishna played with.

Ramkeli - Roop, Sanatan came to see Mahaprabhu

Ramkeli is on the bank of the river Ganga and nearer to the capital of Goud Bengal ruler Hussain Shah. Thousands of people irrespective of caste, creed, religion, languages including street beggars and lepor all came together there to have a glimpse of Lord Sri Chaitanyadev. The place became full of Samkirtan in the name of Lord Sri Krishna whole day and night. Hussain Shah came to know the news. He sent Keshab Khan, an employee of the King's Court to confirm the fact. He after seeing Mahaprabhu and His emotion in devotion of Lord Sri Krishna all the time went back and gave report Hussain Shah it would be better not to disturb the monk from whom no sign of any danger for the Kingdom is expected. There came Roop and Sanatan. They were as Dabir Khas and Sagir Mullick in the court of Hussain Shah. The titles were allotted by Hussain Shah. Their original names were Santosh and the elder Amar. Mahaprabhu awarded Dabir Khas and Sagir Mullick names as Roop and Sanatan. Assuming variable moods of the King Sri Roop through secret messenger advised Sri Chaitanyadev not to stay at Ramkeli nearer to the Capital more and not to start for Mathura Vrindavan as the ways may not be favourable for travel.

Sri Chaitanyadev on way to return Puri - at Shantipur

Sri Chaitanyadev started to return Puri the place of Lord Jagannath. His journey on foot towards Neelachal-Puri was by the side of the river Ganga and He reached the house of Adwaitacharya at Shantipur. Five years' old child of Adwaitacharya, Achyutananda greeted Mahaprabhu first and He took him in His arms. In later days this child became an important personality among the followers of Lord Sri Chaitanyadev and became a disciple of Gadadhar Pundit.

Yata Chaitanyer priya paarishadgan,
Achyuter priya nahey heno naahi jana,

Nityananda swaruper praanera samaan,
Gadadhar Punditera sishyera pradhan. (102)

Adwaitacharya arranged to bring Sachimaa from Nabadwip to Shantipur. Then Sachimaa was like a lunatic woman as she questioned everyone she met the different situation of Lord Sri Krishna at Mathura. To see Mother at Adwaitacharya's house Sri Chaitanyadev fell at the feet of Mother Sachidevi and confessed that no one can pay up the debts of a mother. She took the charge of cooking for Sri Chaitanyadev and prepared various items of fry, shak and other vegetables, as Mahaprabhu Sri Chaitanyadev preferred.

At Kumarhatta

Mahaprabhu Sri Chaitanyadev arrived at Sribaas's house at Kumarhatta. This is the Birth Place of Ishwarpuri. Sribaas expressed his tremendous joy to have Sri Chaitanyadev at his residence. There came father-like Purandar Acharya, came Basudev Dutta, Sibananda Sen and many other devotees and followers. All made the house full of Samkirtan. Sri Chaitanyadev praised highly Basudev Dutta and Ramai Pundit.

Mahaprabhu felt the deplorable pecuniary condition of Sribaas. He knew that Sribaas cannot ask for anything of livelyhood from anybody or to go outside at disciples' houses for earning. He preferred to stay at home and to read the Bhagawat, sing for Lord Sri Krishna and Lord Sri Chaitanyadev the whole of the days. Mahaprabhu Sri Chaitanyadev advised Ramai and other followers to look after Sribaas so that he can chant the name of God without having any anxiety for earning bread and clothes for the members and guests of the family. All agreed to look after this aspect and gave assurance to Mahaprabhu Sri Chaitanyadev. Mahaprabhu could realize this hard reality and tried to solve the problems with other fellowmen.

Mahaprabhu at Panihati

Mahaprabhu alongwith the followers at Panihati on the bank of the river Ganga (nearest Railway station Sodepur). Here resides Raghav Pundit. Getting Mahaprabhu suddenly at his house Raghav Pundit became overwhelmed with joy and devotion. Mahaprabhu told all there-

"Gangayay majjan koiley ye santosh hai
Sei sukh pailaam Raghav alaya." (103)

Raghav Pundit cooked food as preferred by Mahaprabhu himself and Mahaprabhu with his associates accepted the Prasad of Lord Radharaman with joy. Mahaprabhu was much pleased to find profound devotion in Raghav Pundit.

Thousands of people from different sides assembled at the place. Came Purander Pundit, Parameswar Pundit, Raghunath Vaidya, and another Gadadhar known as Das Gadadhar from nearer Ariadah. Das Gadadhar was one of the beloved followers of Lord Chaitanyadev and thereafter became an important associate of Nityanandaprabhu. Here came Makardhwaj whom Mahaprabhu advised to look after Raghav Pundit so that he can bear the expenditure of service offered to devotees and followers from time to time. Mahaprabhu Sri Chaitanyadev expressed his sense of reality as shown in the house of Sribaas at Kumarhatta. Mahaprabhu here advised the Pundit to obey Nityananda as he obeys Him. Thus, Mahaprabhu established Nityananda at Rghav Pundit's house at Panihati.

From Raghav Pundit's house at Panihati Nityananda's glory of spreding Harinaam to all categories of people of the society in the line of Mahaprabhu's thoughts and desires started. Since then Panihati gained the importance like Nabadwip. People would call as second Nabadwip.

At Barhanagar

After Panihati, Mahaprabhu Sri Chaitanyadev reached at Barhanagar, now called Baranagar, on the bank of the Ganga. Here lived Raghunath Pundit, a disciple of Gadadhar Pundit. He listened the recitation of the Bhagabata read by the house owner and received immense joy. He sang and danced almost the whole of the night. Mahaprabhu declared him "Bhagabatacharya". Now the house is known as Pathbari to all.

Sri Chaitanyadev returned at Neelachal

Mahaprabhu Sri Chaitanyadev returned at Neelachal the place of Lord Jagannath and said staring at Gadadhar Pundit that for his attraction He could not proceed to Mathura and Vrindavan.

Pundit Gadadhar's delight to see back Mahaprabhu

At His return Pundit Gadadhar got much delight and at the same time felt sorrow as Mahaprabhu Sri Chaitanyadev could not travel in Mathura-Vrindavan despite He had an intention.

Gadadhar smilingly replied- Wherever you stay the place becomes Vrindavan. All the pilgrims including the Yamuna, the Ganga reach there to grace your presence'.

Gadadhar Pundit consoled Mahaprabhuthat it is true that for teaching others in the country Mahaprabhu is to travel but the rainy season is about to start within a few days. In rainy season the roads become full of water, rivers become furiously over flooded. Therefore, it is better to perform a journey after the rains. During this four months gap Mahaprabhu can maintain Chaturmasya in Puri. All the followers who were present there admitted Pundit Gadadhar's advice to Lord Chaitanyadev and He could not rule out the suggestion given by Gadadhar. On hearing the news that Lord Chaitanyadev would stay in Puri for the next four months all the people at Puri and the King Prataprudra got excited in joy.

Gadadhar invited Sri Chaitanyadev to receive Prasad

Gadadhar invited Mahaprabhu Sri Chaitanyadev to receive Prasd of Tota Gopinath. Mahaprabhu accepted the invitation with all of His other associates present in Neelachal.

"Vikshaatey Punditera Sneha Prabhur Aaswadan
Maanusher Shaktye Dui Naa Hoi Barnan." (104)

Krishnadas Kaviraj explained holy situation of Gadadhar's love and respect to Lord Chaitanyadev and His tasting Prasad both cannot be explained in full by a mortal man on this universe.

Mahprabhu at last travelled in Mathura Vrindavan

Mahprabhu at last traveled in Mathura Vrindavan and He visited the Shiva Place at Varanasi (Kashidham), Prayag etc. on His both the ways of travelling towards and returning. The descriptions of His travelling differ from writer to writer. Especially the descriptions of Krishnadas Kaviraj and Vrindavandas differ. Therefore, we can cite only one description wherein Sri Nityananda's references are available.

According to the writings of Vrindavandas in the Sri Chaitanya Bhagawat Sri Chaitanyadev moved towards Mathura Vrindavan via Kumarhatta at Sribaas's house. The house became full of Samkirtan with thousands of followers and devotees.

Ebe ichchha hoilo Prabhura yaitey Vrindavaney,
Roop-Sanatan-adi yata Bhaktaganey,

Adwaitera haatey dhari bolen Narayan,
Nabadwip diya yabo Vrindavan. (105)

On Way to Mathura-Vrindavan in Shantipur

In Shantipur at Adwaitacharya's house, He met mother Sachidevi for the last time. He requested Adwaitacharya and Sribaas to look after mother Sachidevi.

Seikshaney Sachi loiyan Prabhu Nityananda,
Aailen Prabhur sthaney hoiya ananda,

Sachirey dekhiya Prabhu Sri Gourangaroy,
Pradakshin kori dharey jananira paaya,

Tobe Prabhu Adwaitera haathey dhari bole,
Aamaar janani lagey toma savakarey,

Adwait-Sribaaser haathey sanpiya janani,
Prabhatey gaman koila nyasi-siromani. (106)

At Khardah Nityananda to settle in family life

Then He came to Khardah. He liked the people and the place and advised Nityananda Prabhu to settle there by marrying Basudha and Janhaba:-

Raha Adhikari Hoi Taraha Jagatey
Ichcha ye Kariba Bibha-Milibo Paschatey
Basudha and Janhaba Naamey Lakshmi Saraswati.
(107)

Thus, Sri Chaitanyadev advised Nityananda Prabhu to shoulder the responsibility of a family person by marrying Basudha and Janhaba daughters of Suryadas Sarkhel.

Earlier Sri Chaitanyadev advised Nityananda Prabhu instead of meeting Him in Puri at regular intervals he should take the charge of continuing the publicity the name of God Sri Krishna among all people irrespective of castes and religions throughout Bengal.

He Arrived at Katwa

Then He arrived at Katwa and the people of Katwa got satisfaction to see Gadadhar Pundit with Sri Chaitanyadev as only Gadadhar Pundit can take proper care of Mahaprabhu and Mahaprabhu likes the company most. Sri Chaitanyadev found there Radhanath, an excellent and well known singer. He asked him to chant some songs for Sri Krishna. Radhanath had no team and instruments with him then but Sri Chaitanyadev aspired it and magically the place became full of sounds of all types of musical instruments and Radhanath started to sing. Thus Sri Chaitanyadev aroused the thousands of people gathered there with chanting Samkirtan.

Savey Gadadhar Prabhur Samhati Rahila,
Suniya Katowar Lok Harashit Haila. (108)

Mahaprabhu with Gadadhar Pundit, Roop and Sanatan Started for Vrindavan

After taking bath in the Ganga there arrieved Roop and Sanatan. Mahaprabhu with Gadadhar, Roop and Sanatan started for Vrindavan.

On their way, they visited many forests, rivers, villages, towns and became joyful by feeling the presence of God Sri Krishna with Sri Radha in everything and everywhere. Sri Chaitanyadev and Sri Gadadhar discussed about some secret things of Lord Radhakrishna and both of them became unconscious for some time and it happened repeatedly.

According to Vrindavan Das Sri Chaitanyadev and Sri Gadadhar Pundit with Roop and Sanatan stayed in Vridavan-Mathura for about five years and visited all the Temples including 84 cosh (1.6 kms. make 1 mile, 2 miles make a cosh) Parikrama (encircling) on foot. Sri Chaitanyadev advised Roop and Sanatan to stay in Vridavan for reviving almost vanished and abandoned Temples and Deities from the jungles and to direct all the leading Vaishnavas at Vrindavan by establishing and writing the Scriptures on various aspects. However, Vrindavan Das's writings do not tell much about details of their stay in Vrindavan-Mathura.

Mahaprabhu Sri Chaitanyadev tought Roop and Sanatan for a period of two months all the essential and secret theories and even the theory 'Sadhya Sadhan Tattwa' that was established during the historic conversation with Roy Ramananda on His way towards Southern part of India.

Many people from different sides came to meet Him. Among them were a Brahmin of Maharashtra. Mahaprabhu met Ballav Bhatta of Aulia Village near Prayag.

Mahaprabhu Sri Chaitanyadev personally educated Sanatan Prabhu so that he with his brothers Sri Roop and Sri Ballav and others can preach properly millions of people of the world the theories of Sri Chaitanyadev and Vaishnavism specially the Goudiya Vaishnav thoughts. Sri Chaitanyadev advised him to frame the theories, rules and regulations all of Vaishnavism with others sent by Him earlier. He also advised them to find the demolished or left or forgotten or hidden Deities and Temples in and around Vrindavan-Mathura. He also advised them to look after all the people and devotees living below the poverty line and the lepors also.

Mahaprabhu Sri Chaitanyadev advised Subuddhi Roy to go to Vrindavan-Mathura and chant the Lord Sri Krishna's name and work for the servie for devotees who will reach there. Subuddhi Roy participated social work and religious work with Sanatan and others in Vridavan-Mathura.

Sri Chaitanyadev Returned in Puri

According Krishnadas Kaviraj's description at Narendra Sri Chaitanyadev returned. He had taken decision to return Neelachal via Jharikhand. In the month of Baishakh (April-May) of 1437 Saka (1515 A.D.) Sri Chaitanyadev reached eighteen nallahs (Atharo Nala) and sent Balabhadra to Puri to give the information to other followers and company of His return. Near the Narendra Sarobar all from Puri came and received Him. Sri Chaitanyadev offered due respect and embraced each and every of His blessed and beloved. There assembled Paramananda Puri, Swarup Damodar, Pundit Gadadhar, Jagadananda, Govinda, Bakreswar, Kashi Mishra, Pradyumna Mishra, Pundit Damodar, Haridas Thakur, Pundit Shankar and many others. Wherever Mahaprabhu goes the place becomes full of chanting the name of Sri Krishna by making the environment with celestial happiness.

15

Sri Chaitanyadev's Neelachal Lila Continues

His Highness King Raja Pratap Rudra aspired to meet Sri Chaitanyadev

Raja Pratap Rudra ruled Orissa from 1497 to 1540. He was son of King Purushottamdev who was son of King Kapileswardev descedant of great King Indradumnya of Surya Bansh. (118 of Gourganoddesh Deepika).

In the Book for elaborating the Branch of Gadadhar Pundit's disciples it is found as

Rajanang Srijutang Rudrang Pratapadyang Subishruttam.
Bandey Gadadhara yato Gouro yeno susebitah.

The King of the whole of Orissa Raja Pratap Rudra aspired to meet Sri Chaitanyadev but no one could make Him agreeable. The followers advised the King to see

Him while He would be completely emerged in the emotion for God. One day Mahaprabhu Sri Chaitanyadev was fully engaged in chanting and dancing being encircled with other devotees the King from the roof of the palace saw Him with utter surprise and noted that His chest is drenched with tears in love for Lord Sri Krishna. Raja Pratap Rudra became overwhelmed and the desire to meet Mahaprabhu Sri Chaitanyadev enhanced. The followers then arranged for his teen aged son to meet Mahaprabhu. Mahaprabhu Sri Chaitanyadev was pleased to see the boy and blessed him. King embraced his fortunate son who received Mahaprabhu's touch and favour direct.

Then during the Angaraag period of Lord Jagannath, Balaram and Subhadra finding Sri Chaitanya's changed daily routine of unwinking looking at Jagannath Prabhu the followers arranged a meeting of the King with Sri Chaitanyadev in the garden of Kashi Mishra's house.

Vishnubhakti chinha Prabhu dekhiya Rajaar,
Utha boli Srihasta angey delen taahaar. (109)

To observe the signs of devotion in the King Mahaprabhu said, - I'm here for Ramananda Roy, Sarbabhoum and you the King". He embraced and blessed Raja Pratap Rudra. Mahaprabhu in Vaishnavism made a bridge between people of high altitude and people of below the poverty line. In later days highly educated personalities like Sanatan-Roop-Jib-Adyait-Gadadhar-Jagadananda, Basudev Mishra-Kashi Mishra-Roy Ramananda-Paramananda all followers admitted the aids and co-operation of the benevolent King.

Mahaprabhu after the King's long praising words advised to chant Sri Krishna naam all the time.

Nirantar kara giya Krishna Samkirtan,
Tomaar rakshita Krishnachandra sadarshan,

Tumi Sarbabhoum aar Ramananda Roy,
Tiner nimitta muin aainu ethaaya. (110)

Gadadhar Pundit in worshipping of Tota Gopinath alone in Puri

Gadadhar Pundit was engaged in worshipping of Tota Gopinath alone in Neelachal. He accepted the Mahaprabhu's advice to stay in Neelachal and worshipping of Tota Gopinath lonely so that he could see and serve his beloved lifelong friend Mahaprabhu. The unmarried, nice looking, modest with sweet voice and amiable nature devotee does know nothing but Lord Sri Krishna and lifetime friend Sri Gouranga-Mahaprabhu. In every evening either Gadadhar goes to Mahaprabhu or He goes to Gadadhar. Gadadhar Pundit reads the Srimad Bhagabat with melodious voice daily and by listening to Mahaprabhu Sri Chaitanyadev gets emotion and enjoyment as He liked this very much. They both with Swarup Damodar and other followers sing and dance in the name of Lord Sri Krishna. It also was their regular programme.

Gadadhar sanmukhe paren Bhagawat,

Shuniya prakashe Prabhu prembhav jato.

....

Bhagawat pathey Gadadhar Mahasaya,

Damodar, Swaruper Kirtan bishaya. (111)

Gundicha marjan by Sri Chaitanyadev and others

Sri Chaitanyadev was also conscious about cleanliness. One is to look after health of the thousands of people who come to visit Lord Jagannah. One fine morning before the Rathayatra He decided to clean the Gundicha Temple Himself. Parichhas brought one hundred brooms and one hundred pots. Mahaprabhu Himself scrubbed the Seat of Lord Jagannath, the Kitchen, and the Temple. All the devotees present there brought pots after pots of water. Mahaprabhu did not allow Adwaitacharya, Nityananda, Swarup, Bharati and Paramananda Puri but only to supervise the cleaning work.

Premabeshey kahey Prabhu 'Krishna, Krishna' naam,
Ekaley karen premey satajaner kaam. (112)

The Glorious Divine Chariots Yatra

Then on the next fixed day the Divine Chariots yatra started from the main Temple gate. The destination is Gundicha Temple. Mahaprabhu noticed with surprise that the King Pratap Rudra himself is cleansing the way of the Chariots with a golden broom. It made Mahaprabhu overwhelmed with the love for Lord Sri Krishna.

However, the Chariot did not move a single step. Many able bodied persons were engaged for the pulling. The King arranged to bring all the elephants of his possession. They also failed. Mahaprabhu cannot see by mere standing. He called all the devotees irrespective of castes to pull the Chariots. He Himself from back side pushed the Chariot with His head and the Chariot started to move. All the devotees and Mahaprabhu made the way full of Harinaam.

Tobey Mahaprabhu sov hasti ghuchaaila,
Nijaganey Rathera kaachhi taanibarey dila,

Aapni Rathera paachhey theley matha diya,
Harh harh kori Rath chalila dhaaiya (113)

Mahaprabhu Sri Chaitanyadev advised four teams of Kirtaniya to go at the front of the crowd. Mahaprabhu sang and danced. Surprisingly all the people including the King noticed that at a same time Mahaprabhu is dancing and singing at seven places in the long procession. All also saw that Mahaprabhu remains at the front of the procession of the moving Chariot.

Aagey nritya kori chaley Sachira Nandan. (114).

16

Nityananda Prabhu in Goud Banga

Nityananda towards Goud Bengal

Getting Mahaprabhu's advice Nityananda returned in Goud Bengal.

Prabhu boley suno Nityananda mahamati,
Sattar chalaha tumi Nabadwip prati,

Pratigna korilo aami aapnar mukhey,
Murkhya neech daridrey bhaasabo premsukhey. (115)

Mahaprabu wanted to drive out all sorts of differences from the society. This was His main object and so again He told him –

Etekey aamaar bakyey yadi sattya chaao,
Tobey abilambey tumi Goud deshey jaao,

Murkha neech patit dukhita yata jon,
Bhakti diya karo giya sabarey mochan. (116)

Krishnadas Kaviraaj also confirmed Sri Chaitanya's advice to Nityananda thus –

Nityanandey agnaa dilo – yaaha Goud deshey,
Anargal prembhakti koriha prakashey,

Ramdas Gadadhar adi kathojaney,
Tomaar sahaya laagi dilo toma saney. (117)

Another Devotee Gadadhar known as Dasgadadhar

Dasgadadhar, was an associate of Sri Chaitanyadev and followed Nityanandaprabhu as Mahaprabhu advised. We should note this Gadadhar as in the above sloka was Dasgadadhar (not at all Pundit Gadadhar). Pundit Gadadhar was simply called as Gadadhar or Gadai and he came in Neelachal with his lifetime friend Sri Chaitanyadev. He remained in Neelachal for service to Tota Gopinath and to have direct contacts everyday with Mahaprabhu as usual.

Nityanandaprabhu returned in Goud Bengal

Nityanandaprabhu returned with all his followers in Goud Bengal. He took the responsibility of preaching Sri Krishna naam to all the poor, the rich, educated or illiterates irrespective of castes, religion, language, whatever differences people had then. This was one of the prime motto of Mahaprabhu Sri Chaitanyadev. He escalated the movement and brought the flood of Harinaam in Goud Bengal, Tripura, Assam, and even at the hills area.

Nityanandaprabhu's Followers

On way of return sometime Ramdas engrossed with love for Gopal and remained as tri-broken body. Sometime Dasgadadhar became absorbed in the sense of Radha and dances. Raghunath Vaidya danced as Rebati mother of Balaram. Krishnadas and Parameswardas also take part in dance as little children like Gopal-Balaram. Purandar Pundit jums here and there as Angad of the Ramayana. All including Nityananda were so engaed to dance in different roles that they sometime missed the right direction of their ways. However they somehow could reach Panihati.

Nityanandaprabhu at Panihati

At Panihati Nityanandaprabhu arrived at Raghav Pundit's house. There was Makardhwaj Kar with his team. Expert chanter Madhav Ghose with brothers Govinda and Basudev with musical apparatus arrived there. All started to chant Harinaam and the house became full of cheers.

Nityanandaprabhu's coronation at Panihati

While dancing for love of God and Mahaprabhu suddenly Nityanandaprabhu jumped on a kot and advised all to arrange his coronation and Raghav Pundit ordered others to bring the necessary materials. All the devotees started to bring potful holy water of the Ganga and poured on Nityanandaprabhu's head. One person recited the mantra of bathing of Lord. Nityanandaprabhu wore new clothes. Some followers coated his body with sandalwood pastes. One decorated him with nice garland mixed with Tulsi leaf. They decorated the cot with precious ornaments. Nityananda sat on it and Raghav Pundit held an umbrella on his head. All shouted in applause.

Nityanandaprabhu remembered that Sri Krishna under a Kadamba flower tree is playing the eternal flute and he advised to bring a Kadamba flower. But the season was not favourable for a single Kadamba flower if at all any tree is available nearer. Nityanandaprabhu told Raghav Pundit that it is in his compound and he should enquire minutely. Magically Pundit found many Kadamba flowers on a Pomelo tree in yard of the house. Raghav Pundit made a garland with the flowers and decorated Nityanandaprabhu with it. He once received Mahaprabhu's advice to consider Nityanandaprabhu as Mahaprabhu in His absence. So it was his duty to serve to Nityanandaprabhu as per Lord Sri Chaitanya advised.

Nityananda believed that Mahaprabhu was present among all to witness his crowning ceremony. Therefore, he advised everyone to chant Harinaam all the time. Thus, Panihati for a period of three months remained full of Harinaam.

> Aeirupey Panihati gramey tin maas,
> Nityanandaprabu korey bhaktira vilas. (118)

Nityanandaprabhu's Ornament Ceremony at Panihati

During the period one day, Nityanandaprabhu desired to wear ornaments. The devotees from near and distant places came forward to decorate their Netaichand with huge amount of precious ornaments. Like coronation programme this ornament ceremony has made a history for Panihati.

Once Nityanandaprabhu took the Gopal Deity from Gadadhardas's house at Ariadah and danced for love for Sri Krishna and Sri Chaitanyadev.

Raghunathdas of Saptagram met Nityanandaprabhu

Raghunathdas of Saptagram of Hooghly district was only inheritor of father Gobardhan and soulless elder uncle Hiranya zeminders of bigger areas. But, Raghunath once expressed his desire to become Sannyasi to Sri Chaitanyadev at Shantipur. Mahaprabhu then advised not to hurry to be a Sannyasi but obey the desire of Parents and continue the family life without any attachments. Now having heard that Mahaprabhu has returned from Mathura-Vrindavan he came to Panihati to convince Nityanandaprabhu so that he could easily get Mahaprabhu's darshan. The paternal royal wealth and a beautiful wife could not pull Raghunathdas. Coming over Panihati Raghunath bowed to Nityanandaprabhu.

The Chirah Festival at Panihati as Ordered by Nityanandaprabhu

Seeing him Nityanandaprabhu laughingly said to him - I have got you'. And ordered - now accept the punishment that like a thief you have earlier met Mahaprabhu. O.K. Arrange curd and flattened rice for all the devotees here". He received this orders with pleasure. He with the help of his men brought huge amount of flattened rice, milk, curd, sandesh, sugar and many bananas at Panihati. Thousands of devotees and ordinary people of different castes assembled from different corners of sourrounding districts. More and more sweets, curd, milk, bananas, chirah (flattened rice) were brought within short time. Nityanandaprabhu sat on a platform, on the bank of the Ganga. Seven big pots full of all materials were placed before him. Raghav Pundit from inside came at the spot on the bank of the Ganga and informed Nityanandaprabhu that at his house the puja of Radharaman has been completed, now is the time of taking Prasad. Nityanandaprabhu replied that they would take the Prasad at night and told him to join the Chirah Mahotsav now. There were present Ramdas Thakur, Sundarananda, Dasgadadhar, Murari, Kamalakar Piplai, Sadashiva, Purandar, Dhananjay, Jagadish, Parameswardas, Mahesh, Gouridas, Horh Krishnadas, Uddharan Dutta with his company, many more Brahmins and people of all castes. Raghav Pundit and Raghunathdas were present there to serve Nityanandaprabhu. Nityananda after having felt the Divine presence of Lord Sri Chaitanyadev ordered all to to take the Prasad.

People having failed to find any vacant place to stand took shelter on the river Ganga to take the Prasad of Chirah Mahotsav.

In the evening at Raghav Pundit's house all started the Samkirtan enthusiastically. Then Raghunathdas through Raghav Pundit placed his desire that he wanted to meet Lord Sri Chaitanyadev only if Nityanandaprabhu gives the necessary permission.

Nityanandaprabhu Travelled on both sides of the Ganga

Nityanandaprabhu travelled the villages on the both sides of the Ganga to distribute Harinaam. Nityanandaprabhu once opted to meet Sachimaa in Nabadwip and started for Nabdwip. He reached on way at Khardah nearest to Panihati and there he passed some days at Purandar Pundit's house with Samkirtan. From there he arrived at Triveni where three rivers the Ganga, the Yamuna and the undercurrent Saraswati flow. Here seven rishis got Sri Krishna's grace after Sadhana. He bathed there and went to Uddharan Dutta's house. He visited all other traders' houses, there at Saptagram where maximum number of traders resided. There he sang and danced for love to Lord Sri Chaitanyadev and for Lord Sri Krishna. He went to Ambua area without any hinderance and unlimited love and affection from the people of other religion. Then he arrived at Shantipur at Adwaitacharya's house and was welcomed cordially.

Nityanandaprabhu at Nabadwip

Days passed with Samkirtan and dance led by Nityanandaprabhu. Afterwards he arrived at the feet of Jagatjanani Sachimaa in Nabadwip and at first bowed his head to her. In Nabadwip Nityanandaprabhu resided at Hiranya pundit's house and roamed at the houses of other people.

One miscreant Brahmin by caste found him with precious ornaments on his body and that made him greedy. He posed as a devotee and a perfect and sincere follower of Nityanandaprabhu. After sometime he planned with some more miscreants to rob Nityanandaprabhu as he resided in house alone at night. The gang with arms waited for late night. After a few hours at night Nityanandaprabhu went to bed for sleeping at Hiranya Pundit's house. The miscreants mentally made decision who would take what ornaments after robbing. They all fortunately slept in the bushes as Nityanandaprabhu slept in the house. They woke up with thousands of mosquito bites when Nityanandaprabhu woke up at the dawn by chanting loudly Harekrishna Mahamantra. They being disappointed took unusual early bath in the Ganga and returned to their respective houses.

Next night after worshipping the goddess of power, Maa Chandi they wearing blue dress arrived near Hiranya's house and found that Nityanandaprabhu already was sleeping. They became highly inspired to rob a man helplessly sleeping alone. Surprisingly they noticed that, a group of armed forces having garlands around their necks and Hrinaam in the lips were engaged in guarding the house. They discussed and guessed among themselves that perhaps some rich merchant has come to meet Nityanandaprabhu and so he has brought the guards. But how many days a follower can stay with Prabhu leaving business, property and family? Yet, they are to wait for some more days.They consoled themselves that within a few days these guards would go back with the imagined follower. The deceitful Brahmin devotee advised all of the gang to find every night when Nityanandaprabhu would be alone and then they should take the chance of robbing and till that night they should have patience.

One night they got the scope and utilized it by entering into the house. But nobody could see anything and so all fell in ditches or on thornful bushes. They were also drenched with heavy shower with storm of cold wind. At last all surrendered to Nityanandaprabhu.

Kripamaya Nityananda avatar,
Suni karilen dasyaganer uddhaar.
Again Nityanandaprabhu said to them –
Patitpawan karan hetu Chaitanya Gossain,
Avatari aachhen ihatey anya naai,
Suno dwija yatek paatak koilee tui,
Aar yadi na koris sov nimu muin,
Parahinsa daka churi sov anachaar,
Chharo giya iha tumi na kariha aar. (119)

Sri Chaitanya Mahaprabhu on the behave of Nitynandaprabhu

Once one Brahmin fellow attracted to Sri Chaitanya Mahaprabhu went to Puri to visit Lord Jagannath-Balaram-Subhadra and Sri Chaitanyadev. Puri is also a tourists' attraction spot for the beautiful Sea and the Seabeach. One day finding Mahaprabhu alone he lodged a complaint against Nityanandaprabhu that he does not maintain his life like a perfect Vaishnav. He wears richly dresses, uses richly fragrant cosmetics, decorate himself with precious ornaments and above all does not care for selected food etc. Mahaprabhu smilingly replied that Nitynanda has the right to do anything because he can digest all the situations-

Grihniyaad yavanipaaning visheda ba shoundikalalayam,

Tathapi brahamano bandyong Nityanandapadambujam. (120)

Mahaprabhu convinced him not to judge Nityananda by seeing his outer manners or behaviors but to feel his inside. Try to listen to him what he says to other to observe and do it accordingly. A leaf of Lotus flower can contain drops of water but it does not become drenched itself. Mahadeva Shiva tried to swallow a pot of poison and kept it in His neck. Man cannot do it. He advised him not to consider Nityananda an ordinary man.

Mahaprabhu advised that Brahmin person only to obey the words spoken by the respectables but not to follow everything from their lifestyles.

17

Again, Nityanandaprabhu in Neelachal

Again, Nityanandaprabhu Arrived in Neelachal

Again, Nityanandaprabhu arrived in Neelachal to see Mahaprabhu. It is true that Mahaprabhu advised him not to come in Neelachal frequently but to perform the responsibility to unite and to preach millions of people of Goud Bengal in the name of Lord Sri Krishna. Nityanandaprabhu engaged himself in the work as per Mahaprabhu's advice. However, Nityanandaprabhu cannot find happiness without Mahaprabhu's Divine darshan and direct contacts. He could not resist himself of having a darshan of Lord Sri Chaitanyadev. And so, after bowing to Sachimaa he started for Neelachal with a big team.

Understanding that Sri Nityananda is coming to Neelachal, Sri Chaitanyadev alone came down to

Kamalpur and received him cordially. There He met older Sri Adwaitacharya also.

Then finding Mahaprabhu alone at Kamalpur Nityananda was surprised and both of them embraced each other. Nityananda confessed that as Mahaprabhu drives he dances.

Tomaar nartak aami nachaao ye roopey,
Seiroop naachi aami tomaar koutukey. (121)

Mahaprabhu noticed signs of nine kinds of devotion as explained in the Bhagawat by Prahlad on Nityananda's body, not the precious ornaments and considered his followers as the Gopa *Balak Sakha* like Sridam-Sudam of Vrindavanlila. Mahaprabhu described his wearing the ornaments as Shiva Shankar the great wore snake around His neck is not easily understandable by men as ordinary practices.

Thousands of Spectators from Goud Bengal and Adjacent States

The days of the yatra of the glorious Chariot came at door. As per Mahaprabhu's advice thousands of spectators are coming from Goud Bengal and adjacent states. Adwaitacharya, Pundarik Vidyanidhi for whose coming Mahaprabhu was crying and waitng and Gangadas Pundit his teacher at the begining remained at the front of the team with plenty of enthusiasm and joy. Kirtan performer Bakreswar Pundit, with whom Nrisingha Avatar talks, Pradyumna Brahmachari, beloved devotee Haridas, Basudev Dutta, Mukunda Dutta the singers all were on the way to Neelachal.

The Members of the Teams for Neelachal

Sibananda Sen has the experience of touring Neelachal and he every year on the occasion of the Rathayatra arranges all the necessities of the devotees who wish to have darshan of Jagannath Prabhu and Sri Chaitanyadev at Neelachal. The team was also comprised of other than Sibananda Sen, Raghav Pundit, Makardhwaj Pundit, Govindananda, Govinda Dutta, akhaariya Sri Vijoydas, pure mind Sadashiva Pundit, Purushottam, Sanjay, Sriman Pundit, Nandan Acharya, Suklambar Brahmachari, Krishnadas, Sridhar, writer Pundit Bhagawandas, Gopinath Pundit, Srigarva Pundit, Banamali Pundit, Srihal, Jagadish Pundit, Hiranya Bhagawat, Buddhimanta Khan, Sriacharya Purandar, Murari Gupta as physician, Garurai Pundit, Gopinath Sinha, Sriram Pundit, Narayan Pundit, Sripundit Damodar and the members of the families of hundreds of devotees from Goud Bengal.

Mahaprabhu received all devotees at Atharo Nallah

In one occasion of the coming of the devotees, Mahaprabhu received them at Atharo Nallah. There at Narendra Sarobar at that time, the devotees of the Temple were on the service of Lord Jagannathprabhu-Balaramprabhu-Subhadra Devi on boat. The devotees of Goud Bengal including Sri Chaitanyadev were delighted and they all started to play in the water by spraying water on each other and chanted the glory of Lord Sri Krishna-Lord Jagannath there.

Ragava's Jhali from Panihati (Sodepur)

There were three persons carrying the Ragava's Jhali from Panihati (Sodepur).

Raghav's Jhali was prepared with all types of dried delicious food, pickles, sauce, sweet drops, various fries, as preferred by Sri Chaitanyadev for a year by Raghava's sister Damayantidevi. Raghav Pundit with three porters carry the Jhali to Neelachal every year.

After handing over the Jhali to the associates of Sri Chaitanyadev like Govinda, Jagadananda, Swarup Damodar and others and having met Lord Sri Chaitanyadev at Kamalpur Raghav and others all ran towards the Temple of Lord Jagannath, Balaram and Subhadra to offer due respect.

Sri Nityananda ran to Sri Gadadhar Pundit at Tota Gopinath

Thereafter Sri Nityananda ran to Sri Gadadhar Pundit at Tota Gopinath. They had unthinkable attraction for each other. Their attraction to each other cannot be measured by men but by God Himself. The most polite and disciplined Sri Gadadhar Pundit always remains in deep thought of God Lord Sri Krishna and Lord Sri Chaitanyadev in heart and does the worship of Lord Gopinath Deity as directed by Mahaprabhu. Vrindavandas described –

"Jai Jai Prabhu Sri Gourasundara,

Jai Nityananda Gadadharer Jiban" (122)

Again, Vrindavandas (Central Part 1st Chapter) bowed his head by saying Sri Chaitanyadev is the 'Premadham' of Sri Gadadhar and Sri Adwait Prabhu.

He also described (Central Div 3rd Chap.) Sri Chaitanyadev as Lord of Nityananda and Gadadhar.

Sri Nityananda, Sri Gadadhar and Sri Chaitanya tied in Loving Relation

Sri Nityananda reached the place at the Temple of Gopinath where Gadadhar Pundit is busy with the materials for worshipping of Tota Gopinath with immense absorption in ecstasy. Sri Gadadhar finds Sri Nityananda at the door. They bowed their heads to each other. Both embraced with chests each other for a long time and cried for God Sri Krishna.

Nityananda Gadadharey ye priti antarey,

Taaha kahibar shakti Ishwar se dharey. (123)

Nityananda-Gadadhar love cannot be explained by anybody except by God Himself. Tears from the four eyes flew unendingly. Vrindavandas wrote this occasion-

"Bahjyagnan naahi dui Prabhur sareerey,

Dui Prabhu bhaasey bhakti ananda saagarey."
(124)

Sri Nityananda brought with him one mund (quintal) of fine rice and colored dress for Lord Gopinath. Gadadhar Pundit cooked the rice and thereafter offered the food to Lord Gopinath Deity. After worshipping, they were just ready to take Prasad and then heard from the door the call of Lord Sri Chaitanyadev-

"Gadadhar, Gadadhar, daakey Gourchandra,

Sambhramete Gadadhar bandye Padadawnda."
(125)

Sri Chaitanyadev laughingly said-I, I am not separated soul from you the two. If necessary, I shall establish my rights by force to have the Prasad.'

"Nityananda drabya Gopinather Prasad,

Tomaar randhan eethe aachhe mor bhag." (126)

It is a great fortune for them that Himself Lord Sri Chaitanyadev has appeared at the place. Sri Nityananda and Sri Gadadhar Pundit were overwhelmed to get Lord Sri Chaitanyadev with them, they took Prasad along. The cooking was so delicious that Mahaprabhu praised Sri Gadadhar Pundit as he cooked in his earlier appearance as Radha in Baikunthadham.

"Bujhilam Baikunthey ranna karo tumi,

Tabe aar apanakey lukao ba keni." (127)

Gadadhar Pundit's Divine Glance is necessary to understand Nityanandaprabhu

Again, Vrindavandas wrote that Gadadhar Pundit looks gladly at whom only he can understand Nityanandaprabhu and the person who in mind has the glory for Nityanandaprabhu he knows that it was possible as Gadadhar empowered him. Thus, the Trio Chaitanya-Nityananda-Gadadhar live along and wander in Neelachal -

"Gadadhar subhadrishti karen jahare,

Se jaanite pare Nityananda swarupere.

Nityananda swarupe jaahaar priti money,

Lowaen Gadadhar jaanen sei joney.

Henamate Nityananda Prabhu Neelachaley,

Biharen Gourchandra saungey kutuhaley.

Tinjan ekatra thaken nirantar,

Srikrishna Chaitanya-Nityananda-Gadadhar."

(128)

Mahaprabhu preferred Gadadhar Pundit's Bhagawat reading and Swaroop Damodar's Kirtan

Gadadhar Pundit an unmarried, nice looking, modest with sweet voice and amiable nature devotee who does know nothing but Lord Sri Krishna and lifetime friend Mahaprabhu Sri Chaitanyadev. In every evening, either Gadadhar Pundit goes to Mahaprabhu or He goes to Gadadhar's place. Because Sri Gadadhar reads the Srimad Bhagawat with melodious voice daily and by listening to the reading Mahaprabhu Sri Chaitanyadev got extreme emotion and enjoyment as He liked this friend and his reading the Bhagawat very much. They both with Swaroop Damodar and other followers sing and dance in the name of Lord Sri Krishna. It was their almost a regular programme.

"Gadadhar sanmukhe paren Bhagawat,

Shuniya prakashe Prabhu prembhav jato.

....

Bhagawat pathey Gadadhar Mahasaya,

Damodar, Swaruper Kirtan bishaya." (129)

Among Mahaprabhu's two best preferences one was to listen Srimad Bhagawata from the melodious voice and appropriate narration read and discussed by Gadadhar Pundit and the another was to listen and enjoy the Kirtan sang and elaborately discussed by Swarup Damodar.

Sachimaa's Love for God

Once Mahaprabhu enquired to Damodar Swrup, on his return from Nabadwip whether Sachimaa is alright in Nabadwip and got sharp reply that she was always absorbed in love for Lord Sri Krishna. Mahprabhu answered –

Yata kichhu Vishnubhakti sampatti aamaar,
Aira prasadey sov dwidha naahi taar. (130)

Without Bhakti Nothing is Fruitful

He also said, without Bhakti nothing is fruitful. Money, fame, property everything would become useless, useless for the society.

There was Keshav Bharati present and he echoed the saying by reminding all that Brahma, Shiva, Narada, Prahlad, Vyas, Sukhdev, Sanaka brothers, Yudhisthir, Priyabrata, Prithu, Dhruba, Akrur, Uddhav and the other Mahajanas opted the Bhakti only to Lord Sri Krishna.

Mahajano yena gatah sau panthaah. (131)

Thousands of the Devotees in Puri

Thousands of the devotees assembled in Puri on the occasion of the glorious Rathayatra. Everyday all devotees of Goud Bengal and other places after having darshan of Lord Jagannath-Balaram-Subhadra in the Temple attend at Gambhira to have a darshan of Mahaprabhu Sri Krishna Chaitanya.

Many devotees bring some materials for Mahaprabhu's eating and using. Govinda keeps as per Mahprabhu's direction. On another day, Govinda places all the accumulated eating gifts at His front and announces evrybody's name and Mahaprabhu receives all the gifts at a time. Govinda gets relief that he can answer suitably to all Devotees who may enquire the fate of their gifts to Mahaprabhu.

Many Desired to offer alms to Mahaprabhu at their Puri Residence

Some of them desired that Mahaprabhu would accept alms at their temporary residence in Puri. Mahaprabhu cannot receive everybody's invitation as their number were much more of the days of their staying there. Moreover there were some fixed days booked for offering alms to Mahaprabhu by Gadadhar Pundit and Sarbabhoum-

Gadadhar Pundit, Bhattacharya Sarbabhoum,
Inhaa sovaar aachhey bhikshadivas niyam. (132)

Mahaprabhu would Accept Invitation only from the Lakshapati

Therefore, Mahaprabhu announced that only from the Lakshapati He would accept invitation for alms. All were surprised that Mahaprabhu for all. He loves all irrespective of castes and financial abilities. He loves the King of Orissa and other rich devotees and also ordinary banana cone seller Sridhar and almost known as beggar Suklambar Brahmachari. Then how He could frame a rigid regulation that He would not accept invitation from a person who is not a Lakshapati?

All got answers within a few days that he would be considered as Lakshapati only who chants or take Lord Sri Krishna's name in rosary one lakh times a day.

Mahaprabhu Sri Chaitanyadev Himself is Lord Sri Krishna

To thousands of devotees' belief Mahaprabhu Sri Chaitanyadev is Lord Sri Krishna in the Kaliyug and one day, sang-

Jai Jai dwijaraj baikuntha behari,
Jai Jai sarva jagatera upakari,

Jai Krishna Chaitanya Sri Sachira Nandana,
Ei mata gai naachey sata sankhya jana. (133)

Mahaprabhu felt embarrassed. Sribaas said it was a spontaneous chanting and who would stop whom, everybody believes that Mahaprabhu Sri Chaitanyadev is Lord Sri Krishna Himself in the Kaliyug. Sribaas replied –

Sri Baas bolen Prabhu ebe ki karibaa,
Sakal sansar guy kotha lukaiba. (134)

And others like Nityananda, Adwait, Swarup, Gadadhar have the same opinions –

E hena se Chaitanyadev bhaktabatsal,
Ihaaney Sri Krishna kori gayaena sakal,
Sovey boley Sri Krishna Chaitanya Bhagawan. (135)

Prabhati Kirtan

Every early morning all the devotees present for the four months in Puri chant Harinaam and the name of Mahaprabhu and roam in the town. Sometime they sang–

Bhajo Krishna, Laha Krishna, Kaha Krishna naamrey,
Ye jan Krishna bhajey Se hoi aamaar pranrey.

Sometime some sang-

Bhajo Gouranga, Laha Gouranga, Kaha Gourangera naamrey. Ye jana Gouranga bhajey se hoi aamaar pranrey. (136)

Personal Emotion for Everyone

Every year all the devotees assemble in Puri on the occasion of the glorious Rathayatra and meet Mahaprabhu at Gambhira during the four months of rains and one day their time of return comes. All become gloomy in mind. They do not want to leave Mahaprabhu but the hard reality of the familymen force them to return. Sri Chaitanyadev also gets ache in heart and tears come out from His eyes. He embraces each and every and tells them if possible to visit Puri every year. Feeling Mahaprabhu's affection and love to all, they sometime change their programme of return for more a few days because they all love Mahaprabhu as the most beloved own person.

Tabey Mahaprabhu sovakarey prabodhiya,
Sovarey vidaya dila susthira hoiya,

Nityanandey kahen – Tumi naa aaiso varvar,
Tathai aamaar sanga hoibey tomaar. (137)

Haridas Remained in Puri

Haridas came to Puri and Mahaprabhu did not allow him to return and arranged a little room in the garden nearer to His residence in the house of Kashi Misra. Haridas there used to cite 'Hare Krishna' Mahamantra silently and sometime chant the whole day and night. He tried to complete chanting and citing silently Harinaam three lakh times a day. Sometime it took much more time, so he could not get time to have Prasad brought by Govinda at lunchtime daily. Mahaprabhu used to take Prasad after sending Prasad to Haridas by the hand of Govinda.

One day hearing that Haridas is ill and cannot move or cannot take Prasad Mahaprabhu came to see him. Haridas was thin and lean and crying for he cannot complete three lakh time citing and chanting for Lord Sri Krishna. To see Mahaprabhu Himself attended at the hut Haridas said in low voice that he desires to leave this world before Mahaprabhu. He requested Him to please arrange it.

Haridas left the earth lying on the lap of Lord Sri Chaitanyadev

The next day Lord Sri Chaitanyadev arrived in the hut and took him on His lap. Haridas and other blessed followers started to chant Harinaam and some time later he breathed his last lying on the lap of Lord Sri Chaitanyadev.

Na jaayatey mriyaytey ba kadachinnayang bhuttwa bhabita ba na bhuyah,

Ajo nityah shashwatoayang purano na hanyatey hanyamaaney sharirey. (138)

Again same thing in Upanishad-

Na jayatey mriyatey ba bipaschinnayang kutaschinna babhuva kaschid,

Ajo nityah shashwatoayang purano na hanyatey hanyamaney sharirey. (139)

Mahaprabhu Himself carried the earthly body left by beloved Haridas to the seashore and buried him there. Then Lord Sri Chaitanyadev begged for Prasad to observe obsequies for Haridas. All the devotees including the Her Highness Queen sent lot of Prasad for the ritual. Mahaprabhu for some time remained silent to bear with the shock for one of the most pure and most beloved devotees Haridas's demise. He knew that-

Yashmin sarvani bhutani aatmaibabhud vijanatah,

Tatra ko mohah kah shoka ekatwamanu-pashyatah. (140)

After all Mahaprabhu appeared in human body

Still His shock was natural, after all Mahaprabhu appeared in human body on this earth for love, love to all i.e. love to Sri Krishna. Haridas was His own man and He considered him as His elder one in taking the name of Lord Sri Krishna from the very beginning.

Mahaprabhu possessed by deepest feeling in love for Lord Sri Krishna

Mahaprabhu becomes thin day after day as He all the time remain in love for Lord Sri Krishna and cries silently sometime loudly for Lord Sri Krishna. Being much engrossed in love for Radhakrishna of Vrindavan, He sees the Eternal Divine Lila in His mind and sometime at His front. So, in order to cash Radhakrishna He fell into a well. He runs to the Chatak hill thinking it the

Gobardhana that Lord Sri Krishna held in His little finger of the left hand to save the residents of Braja from the hands of Devaraj Indra. Seeing a flower garden He thinking the Vrindavan runs towards it to touch Lord Sri Krishna. The colour blue of water of the sea appears to Him as colour of Lord Sri Krishna and Mahaprabhu jumps into it. He has no differences of night and day to cry for Lord Sri Krishna and He goes out of the room even guarded by Shankar Pundit who used to sleep at His feet, Govinda, Jagadananda, Swarup Damodar and others.

Sometime he placing His thin body on the shoulder raches the Tota Gopinath where His lifetime friend Gadadhar Pundit reads the Bhagawata daily and somehow comes back Gambhira resting His hands on the shoulders of closed company.

Every year people of the Country attend Rathayatra Festival in Puri

Every year people of Goud Bengal, Tripura and other places of the Country assemble in Puri but day after day Mahaprabhu remains silent and only on the day of the Rathayatra He comes at the front of the mega processions of the glorious Rathayatra. Out of twenty four years after the Sannyas six years passed for trekking in the Country and this state of Mahaprabhu in Gambhira continued for the rest eighteen years.

18

Nityananda as a Social Reformer

Authentic Writings

We can learn little of the life of Nityanandaprabhu from authentic writings. However, Nityananda was the most popular and maximum propagated Hero in building agreat society of Harinaam in Goud Bengal during the last almost 500 years.

No remarkable poet nor a renowned writer has written any sepaperate and remarkable book on complete life of Nityanandaprabhu. The information mainly are available in Sri Chaitanya Bhagawat, Sri Sri Chaitanya Charitamrita and Sri Chaitanya Mangal. Afterwards many books were written by writers all of those can hardly demand authencity. However, mainy Researchers and Critics have collected many information about Nityanandaprabhu. (141)

Nityananda gave shape to Mahaprabhu's Dreams and Aims

Nityanandaprabhu was the main performer of giving shape of Mahaprabhu's dreams, aims and objects. We can understand the social reformation started to flow by Nityanandaprabhu from the Chirah Mahotsav at Panihati (1516 A.D.)

Appearances of Nityanandaprabhu

It is true, Nityanandaprabhu having tied decorated anklets at his feet, wearing a pair of earings, a turban on his head, Neelkantha Mahadeva hanging from neck, keeping Anantadev Shila and Tripurasundari yantra on head tied with taft and having lot of ornaments on whole body danced and sang the Lord Sri Krishna's name. It seemed to be much dramatic, but this dramatic attitudes were sometime required for attracting a large number of ordinary people and all these were for love to Lord Sri Chaitanya as well as for Lord Sri Krishna.

Thus, he overwhelmed all categoris of people. This helped many tradesmen, cultivators, businessmen and even poets-writers to flourish in respective lines. The economy of Goud Bengal got immense help to develop.

Goud Bengal Regained New Life

We can say, Goud Bengal got new life. Poets like Vrindavandas, Krishnadas Kaviraj and others got much inspiration from Nityanandaprabhu to write on Sri Chaitanyadev, Sri Krishna, Sri Ramchandra and on the characters of the Mahabharata and of other Puranas. Ordinary people who could not dare to taste the classic literature they also started to quench their thirsts by reading those writings in vernacular at hand at ease. He eased many things for the people downtrodden or upstars. He travelled with the mission of Harinaam for all at Panihati, Khardah, Nimta, Ariadah, Nityanandatala, Katwa, Kuliya, Ambuya, Badagachhi, Kanchanpalli, Kumarhatta, Uddharanpur, Bakreswar, Ekchakra, Aantisara, Chhatrabhog, Hatiyagarh, Nityanandapur, Patharghata, Tambuli, Pichhalda, Dogachhiya, Khanajora, Triveni, Akna Mahesh, Saptagram, Chaatra, Kotrang, Betor, Burhan, Mayapur, Fuliya, Banidighi, Jaleswar and above all Nabadwip. At all places wherever he himself went thousands of people gathered around him and regained the belief that all are human beings and many of them became Vaishnav.

Organizational Capability

Nityanandaprabhu's organizational capacity was beyond the imagination then. He did all for fulfilling the dreams of Mahaprabhu and he did it for revitalizing the life of Goud Bengal. Sri Chaitanyadev with Adwaitachary, Sribaas, Gadadhar Pundit and other hundreds of follwers established a non-violent democratic society and Nityanandaprabu with his team escalated the movement in Goud Bengal. The seed of democracy without any violence was sowed beneath the earth of Bengal by Sri Chaitanyadev and Nityanandaprabhu gave it shape of a big tree that gave shadow in the Country for the last five hundred years.

Nityanandaprabhu Shouldered the Responsibility

Nityanandaprabhu shouldered the responsibility himself and with the help of his *Dwadasa Gopal*, the twelve of his followers. They were – Ramdas (Abhiram), Gouridas Thakur, Sundarananda, Kala Krishnadas,

Purushottamdas, Uddharan Dutta, Srikammalakar Piplai, Dhananjay Pundt, Mahesh Pundit, Prameswardas, Das Gadadhar and Basudev Gbosh. (In the book Baanglar Kirtan O Kirtaniya ed. Harekrishna Mukhopadhyay mentioned the list of Dwadas Gopal as – Sarvasri Abhiram Thakur, Kamalakar Piplai, Uddharan Dutta, Kala Krishnadas, Gouridas Pundit, Dhananjay Pundit, Parameswardas, Nagar Purushottam, Purushottamdas, Mahesh Pundit, Sridhar and Sundarananda Thakur.)

Upa Gopals and Others

Others, who engaged themselves in the mammoth work of Sri Nityananda as directed by Sri Chaitanyadev of spreadimg Harinaam among all the people at different corners were – Purushottam Kaviraj, Nidhu or Sishu Krishnadas, Veerbhadra Gossain, Madhab Ghosh, Murari Pundit, Raghunath Vaidya, Suryadas Sarkhel, Krishnadas Sarkhel, Purandar Pundit, Jagadish Pundit, Balaramdas, Jadunath Kavichandra, Krishnadas Horeh, Manohar, Devananda, Behari, Nakarhi Mukunda, Surya, Madhabananda, Ramananda Basu, Jagannath, Mahidhar, Srimanta, Gokuldas, Hariharananda, Shibaai, Nandaai, Paramananda Abadhoot, Vasanta, Navin Hore, Gopal, Sanatan, Binchai Hazra, Krishnananda, Sulochan, Kansari Sen, Ram Sen, Ramchandra Kaviraj, Govinda Kaviraj, Sriranga Kaviraj, Mukunda Kaviraj, Pitambar, Madhbacharya, Damodardas, Shankar Mukunda, Jnandas, Manohar, Nartak Gopal, Rambhadra, Gourangadas, Nrisingha Chaitanyadas, Meenketan Ramdas, Vrindavandas and more. Other than the list, some scholars tried to include the names of Halaudh Thakur, Sri Garva Pundit, banana cone seller Sridhar, one of the most beloved devotee by Sri Chaitanyadev, as the pioneers in the team of spreading the Harinaam movement with Sri Nityananda.

There were more persons called as Upa Gopal. Like other Gopal, they also propagated Harinaam among huge number of people of urban and suburban areas of Goud Bengal. With the large organizational set up Sri Nityananda was successful to fulfill the dreams of Lord Sri Chaitanyadev. With the tireless efforts the seed of Equality and Democracy without any violence thus got shape in the hands of the followers of Nityanandaprabhu under direction of Mahaprabhu Sri Chaitanyadev.

Nityanandaprabhu for Famine Stricken People

Once during a famine Sri Nityananda with the help of Uddharan Dutta, Sridhar, Baninath Banik, Srikar Dutta, Taracharan Chakraborty, Navin Horeh and others started a charitable camp for distribution of food to the famine victims near Bandel in the district of Hooghly.

Housing Project for the Shelterless

Nearby Bandel he also arranged a housing project for the shelterless people on the bank of the river Saraswati. That was known as Bhadravan or Vedo.

For Water Crisis

Near Krishnagar at Gatra (Gandivnagar) he arranged a big tank for meet up water crisis.

Nityanandaprabhu and Education System

Sri Nityananda visited many schools to spread the learning of Yogasana and the lessons how to build up human characters of the future generations.

Nityanandaprabhu and the People of Hills Area

He also thought actively for the development of people at Garo Hills in the district Maimansingha (now in Bangladesh). There he got Pathar Hasang with his men.

In Women Freedom

Sri Nityananda was also a pioneer in the Women Freedom movement. He inspired his wife Janhaba Devi to come forward in the front line. Later Janhaba Devi gave her leadership in the historic Kheturi Mahotsav.

Effect on Society

Some researchers assumed that Nityananda married in 1519 A.D. while Sri Chaitanyadev was in full form as Moving Brahma in Puri. After Mahaprabhu, Nityananda got only 12 years (some say 9 years) in hand. But he started the work strongly from Panihati and successfully united the people from Poor to Rich, Illiterate to Enlightened, Chandal to Brahmin irrespective of any differences under an umbrella of Harinaam. Men learnt to honour others as men. Human selfrespect and understanding thus enhanced within a short time. People knew that they are the sons of Amrita "Amritasya Putrah". With this unique unity, people gathered at different occasions, ceremonies and got the scopes of making exchange opinions, own products to each other etc. among each other. Along with social scenario the economic scenario also got its speed towards the path of development. Bengal started to breathe joyfully.

Personal Life of Nityanandaprabhu

According to Bhakti Ratnakar by Narahari Chakraborty (Ghanshyamdas) one Brahmin from Badagachhi reached the house of Suryadas Sarkhel at village Shaligram with a proposal of the marriage. Some said that with the enthusiasm of Kala Krishnadas, or of Rukunpur King Krishnads Horeh and Uddharan Dutta the marriage took place at Shaligram (different opinion, at Saptagram) in 1519 A.D. (different opinion, in 1520 A.D.), (different opinions, in 1533 or in 1534).

He married to Basudha Devi and Janhaba Devi the two daughters of Suryadas Sarkhel of Ambika Kalna in the district of Bardhaman. His son Veerbhadra (Veerchandra) was born in the lap of Basudha Devi. They had one daughter Ganga Devi by name.

Janhaba Devi had no issue. She adopted young Ramchandra. Therefore, Janhaba's son Ramchandra became another son of Nityanandaprabhu. Ramchandra was originally son of Chaitanyadas. Chaitnyadas was son of Bansibadan Chattopadhyay who was resident at Mahaprabhu's house in Nabadwip. Bansibadan's grandson Ramchandra was also a fan of Lord Sri Chaitanyadev and he witnessed the Lila of Mahaprabhu. Ramchandra established Sripat at Baghnapara. Veerachandra (Veerbhadra) after Nityananda became the Life of Sripat Khardah.

After Nityanandaprabhu

Janhaba Devi and the competent son Veerchandra carried the responsibility of Nityanandaprabhu as desire had by Mahaprabhu. Under the leadership of Janhaba Devi there a mega conference of all the Vaishnavas was held in 1581(1583) at Kheturi. The flow of Harinaam Movement introduced by Sri Chaitanyadev and all kainds of developments in every sphere of life of People is still in action as the flow of the Ganga-Brahmaputra-Yamuna-

Godavari-Krishnaa-Cauvery-Narmada-Sindhu-Gomati flow and so on in the most sacred land of Bharatbhumi.

Janhaba Devi's efforts to write all the teams of various branches of Goudiya Vaishnavas got success. Her efforts of making bridge between Vaishnavas of Nabadwip and of Vrindavan was also an important aspect. Let us bow to her.

Homage

We pay our heartiest homage to Lord Sri Chaitanyadev and His lifetime associate Sri Gadadhar Pundit and His commander in chief Sri Nityananda.

In the month of Ashara at Saptami of full moon Sunday (1533 A.D. June) in the after noon Mahaprabhu with tears in eyes for extreme Love for Lord Jagannath, entered into the Temple at Gundicha wherein Prabhu Jagannathdev had been placed after Rathayatra.

He told Gadadhar Pundit to remain outside the Temple. Probably half an hour later Gadadhar was informed that Mahaprabhu has emerged into the Deity of Lord Jagannath and at once Gadadhar rushed into that Temple to find Mahaprabhu and he too did not back from the Temple. In this context Sri Vrindavandas in the Sri Chaitnya Bhagawat had written-

"Gadadharey Boley Prabhu- Shuno Gadadhar,
Aami Aage Jaai Tumi Aashaha Paschatey,"

Mahaprabhu told Gadadhar to listen to Him that He is entering into the Gundicha Temple and advised

Gadadhar Pundit to enter into Temle afterwards. But soon after Gadadhar knew the information of Mahaprabhu's disappearance.

"Gadadhar Jaanilen – Prabhur Gaman,
Prabhur Birahey Tan Na Rahey Jiban,

Achambite Gadadhar Hoila Antardhan,
Naa Paay Dekhitey Keho Boley – Ramah."

Gadadhar Pundit knew that Mahaprabhu has gone and so Gadadhar could not bear the separation from Mahaprabhu any longer and he rushed into the Gundicha Temple. Alas, Suddenly Gadadhar also disappeared. Nobody could realize the mystery.

"Eaimotey Mahaprabhu Gadadhar Loiah,
Nijasthaney Gela Prabhu Antardhan Hoiah," - Thus Mahaprabhu taking Gadadhar with Him disappeared and went His own place of divinity. (142)

The elderly scholar with lot of knowledge and experiences Krishnadas Kaviraj in the Sri Sri Chaitanyacharitamrita preferred not to mention any of the actual happenings whatever these were. He just paid his last salute by bending his head to the readers only and concluded the writing.

"Prabhur Gambhira Lila Naa Pari Bujhitey,
Buddhi-Prabesh Naa pari Barnitey,

Sob Shrota Vaishnaver Bandiya Charan,
Chaitanya Charit Koila Samapan." (143).

It is also hearsay that Swaroop Damodar was found almost dead after bleeding from heart on the road outside the Temple.

In the case of Nityanandaprabhu's leaving this earth, researchers are still awaiting the more authentic information. However, researchers presumed, that in1542 A.D. (some liked to mention it was 1545) Nityanandaprabhu breathed his last at the age of 68 (71) near Panihati or Khardah.

The present author tried to remain confined almost in the two authentic writings of Sri Vrindavandas and Sri Krishnadas Kaviraj.

Thousands of devotees and followers like to believe the spiritual thoughts, activities and consciousness of Lord Sri Chaitanyadeva, Sri Adwaitacharya, Sri Nityanandaprabhu, Sri Gadadhar Pundit, Sribaas, Swarup Damodar and others are deathless. The lives and the preachings for Love to Lord Sri Krishna are immortal forever.

We bend down our heads in homage to Them all.

Please pardon the author if any information found wrong or unsuitable. May God bless all of the readers and devotees. Please pray a bit to Him for the author that he may have the love for Him.

There is No End of Sri Krishnakatha as well as with associates Sri Chaitanyakatha.

Author Acknowledges the Indebtedness

1-4. Sri Chaitanya Charitamritamrita by Krishnadas Kabiraj, Adi Lila Chapter I.

5. Sri Chaitanya Bhagawat by Vrindavandas Adi Khanda Chapter 2.

6. Comments by Dr. Asit Kumar Bandyopadhyay in Goudiya Vaishnav Darshaner Bhumika by Dr. Sukhendu Sekhar Gangopadhyay.

7. Ch. Bh. Adi. Chap. 3.

8. Do Chap.10.

9. Do Chap.11,

10. Ch.Ch. A.i. Chap. XVI.

11. Amiya Nemai Charit 1/8 Mahatma Sisir Kumar Ghosh.

12-13. Ch. Bh. Madhya. Chap. 2 and above.

14. Simad Bhagawata (10/ 23/22).

15-16. Ch. Bh. Madhya. Chap.1.

17 &18. Do. Chap. 2.

19. Do. Chap. 3.

20-21. Do. Chap. 8.

22-23. Do. Chap. 3

24-28. Do. Adi. Chap. 8.

29 to 31. Ch. Bh. Madhya. Chap. 3.

32. Do Chap. 4 and Srimad Bhagawat 10/21/05.

33. Do Chap. 4.

34. Do Chap. 2.

35 - 38. Do Chap. 4.

39.- 43..Do Chap.5.

44. Ch. Ch. Adi. Chap. XVII.

45. as above 39.

46 – 47. Do Chap. 6.

48 – 52. Do Chap. 8.

53. Do Chap. 9.

54. -57. Do Chap.11.

58. Do Chap.12.

59 – 62. Do Chap.13.

63 & 64. Do Chap.16.

65. –67. Do Chap.18.

68 – 69. Do Chap.19.

70. Do Chap. 20.

71 – 72. Do Chap. 21.

73 – 77. Do Chap. 23.

78. Ch. Ch. Adi Chap. 17.

79. Ch. Bh. Madhya. Chap. 24.

80 – 85. Do Chap. 25.

86 – 89. Do Chap. 26.

90. Goudiya Vaishnav Darshaner Bhumika-Sri Chaitanyadev O Bhaktidharma by Dr. Sukhendu Sekhar Gangopadhyay

91. Sri Chaitanya Mongal by Lochandas, Madhya.Chap. 14.

92. Sri Chaitanyadev's Sloka on Yamuna refd. Ch. Ch. Madhya III from Chaitanya Chandradaya natakam.

93. Ch. Bh. Shesh. Chap.1.

94. Ch. Ch. Madhya. Chap. III.

95 – 97. Ch. Bh. Shesh. Chap. 2.

98. Ch. Ch. Madhya. Chap. IV.

99. Do Chap.V

100. Goudiya Vaishnav Sadhana by Harekrishna Mukhopadhyay.

101. Ch. Ch. Madhya. Chap. X.

102. Ch. Bh. Shesh. Chap. 4.

103. Do Chap. 5.

104. Ch. Ch. Madhya. Chap. XVI.

105. Ch. Bh. Shesh Chap.10.

106. Do. 11.

107. Ch. Bh. Shesh. Chap.12.

108. Ch. Bh. Shesh. Chap.11.

109 –10. Do Chap. 5.

111. Do Chap. 9.

112. Ch. Ch. Madhya. Chap. 12.

113-14. Do Chap.13.

115-16. Ch.Bh.Shesh Chap. 5.

116. Ch. Ch. Madhya. Chap. XV .

118 -19. Ch. Bh. Shesh Chap. 5.

120. Do Chap. 6.

121. Do Chap. 7.

122. Do Adi Chap. 2.

123-28. Do Shesh Chap.7.

129. Do Chap. 9.

130-31. Do Chap. 8.

132. Ch. Ch. End Chap. X.

133-35. Ch. Bh. Chap. 8.

136. Author's Book Sri Chaitanyadev O Sri Gadadhar Chap. 17, p. 129.

137. Ch. Ch. End. Chap. XII.

138. Srimad Bhagawatgita Chap.II Sloka 20.

139. Katho Upanishad 1/2/18.

140. Isha Upanishad Sloka No. 7.

141. Writings on Sri Nityananda by Dr. Kanan Behari Goswami, Sanat Kumar Naskar, Jibasharan das, Keshav Aadu, Barid Baran Ghosh and Sri Raghunath Goswami in Manavpremik Nityananda and Bangla Charit Sahityey Nityananda edited and written respectively by Dr. Uma Bandyopadhyay.

142. Ch. Bh. Shesh. Chap.1 .

143. Ch. Ch. End. Chap. XX

and also remains grateful to

1. Srila Mukundalal Goswami, Bhakti Siromani.
2. Srila Bijoy Krishna Goswami (Chanak - Burdwan).
3. Srila Acharya Prabhupad Prankishore Goswami (Sri Gouranga).
4. H.H. Shanthaveera Swamiji (Bangalore)
5. Prabhupad Sri Bejanbehari Goswami, M.A. Shadatirtha, Dip-in-Lib, Bhagawatacharya.
6. Sri Purnenduprasad Bhattacharya (Sahitya Mela), Bharat Bhasha Bhushan.
7. Smt. Bhumika Goswami (Samanawasri - Bhagawatsri).
8. Jyotish Samrat Sri Mantra Bhattacharya.
9. Sri Sankha Bhattacharya (Music World).
10. Sri Satish Chaturvedi (ABBSS - Bhopal).
11. Dr. Bidhan Chandra Biswas (Raganuga).

Sri Chaitanyadev in Touch of Working Class People

Sridhar

Sridhar was an ordinary banana skin and cine seller at an unimportant corner of a market/hat place. At the young age Nemai had a practice to meet him and jokingly bargained for banana skin or cones. Naturally, the place surrounded by villages 500 years back those were almost the cheapest commodities in markets. Nemai knew that this ordinary cone seller was dedicated devotee of Lord Sri Krishna but he never express himself. Nemai liked to bargain with him or sometime forced him to give up all of his residuals without any price saying that he has gained much earlier. Sridhar posing anger on Nemai liked give all the cones and skins of banana as he also saw some hidden Divine Power in him. Later Nemai called Sridhar in the Samkirtan movement. Once at the time of return with His triumphant rally from Kazi's house Nemai known as Sri Gouranga Mahaprabhu being so much more engrossed with love for Lord Sri Krishna that

Mahaprabhu Sri Gourangadev even drank water in the broken iron pot left at the end of the house of Sridhar. Sridhar was one of the mostly beloved and efficient company of Lord Sri Gouranga. A real devotee Sridhar thereafter worked with Sri Nityanandaprabhu during spreading Harinaam among all the people in Bengal.

Nemai at Shuklambar's residence

One morning some devotees of Sri Krishna were plucking flowers and Tulsi leaves for worshipping Sri Krisha at a flower garden. There were present Gadadhar, Gopinath, Ramai, Sri Baas and some others. Sriman Pundit hurriedly came to them. He told them as an announcement, that their Sri Gouranga is changed to a new personality and has become modest one. He does not show any audacity and tease by asking any question to anybody. He becomes mad whenever listens the name of Lord Sri Krishna. He also added that, Sri Gouranga should express the experiences of Gaya tour at Shuklambar's residence in the afternoon and any body could meet the meeting.

In the afternoon Gadadhar took shelter by hiding himself for hearing what Sri Gouranga would say at Shuklambar Brahmachari's residence. Sri Gouranga came to the house with tilting body, as the heart is always full with thoughts of Lord Sri Krishna.

He cries – "Where is Krishna. Krishna was seen here, now where He has gone." Other Krishna followers also feeling Lord Sri Krishna's presence and some were weeping in love for God. Gadadhar Pundit, however, could not restrain his ecstasy. With his head bowed down, he continued to cry very loudly from the hiding place.

Hearing his pitiful sobbing, Sri Gouranga enquired-

'Who is there weeping?'

Murari answered-'It is Gadadhar. Yours Gadadhar.'

Sri Gourangadev called Gadadhar with much affection and Gadadhar leaving the hiding corner came out and fell on the feet of Gourangadev. He told Gadadhar–

'Your life is successful as you are worshipping Lord Sri Krishna from the childhood. Alas, I have wasted the time without worshipping Krishna.' (11)

By saying this, Mahaprabhu Sri Gouranga embraced Gadadhar in great love and again fainted.

The Triumphant Rally returned through the places of the citizens

After the Kazi vijaya Mahaprabhu with thousands of fellow person who joined the triuamphant the Historical Rally traveled at Gadigachha, Payraadaanga, and other localities. All people showered flowers on Mahaprabhu and others. Thus Sri Gouranga Mahaprabhu met all the citizens on His way. He did not bother the casteism or financial position of the people born on this earth.

Mahaprabhu went to everybody's house of Nabadwip

During the peak hours of Harinaam Samkirtan at Sri Baas angan one day Mahaprabhu Sri Gourangadev went to every house of Nabadwip. He met all types of people irrespective of castes, religions and trades. Always Gadadhar, Nityananda, Sri Baas, Haridas, Mukunda,

Murari, Sridhar, Suklambar, Sanjay and many others remained with Him chanting for Lord Sri Krishna. He personally offered due respect to Conch sellers, Essence sellers, Weavers, Pan sellers, Banana cone and stem seller and many others and all the people gave proper regards to Him. All took Him as own person.

Mahaprabhu blessed Suklambar Brahmachari

The Samkirtan became popular day by day with the presence of all the devotees of Lord Sri Krishna. One day there came Suklambar Brahmachari and joined the team. Mahaprabhu found him to sing and dance with others. He was dancing and his belonging a bag also swinging. Mahaprabhu took some handfuls of rice and particles he got from different houses and started to eat those chewing.

Prabhu boley tor khud kon muin khaon,
Abhaktera amrita oolti naahi chaaon.(64)

Mahaprabhu took Prasad in the house of Suklambar Brahmachari

One day Mahaprabhu remembered that once He took handsful of mixes rice from the begging bag of Suklambar Brahmachari. He called him again and told him that Mahaprabhu would take Prasad at his residence. The poor Suklambar arranged for the Prasad. It was as nice and as rich that even sometime a well to do person cannot afford so much arrangements that Suklambar had arranged. As if goddess Jaganmata Lakshmidevi took the entire responsibility to supply necessary food for Mahaprabhu and His all associates at Suklambar's house.

There came one Vijaydas and found Lord Sri Krishna at the seat although there was no Deity in the house of Suklambar Brahmachari.

Ishan a blessed person at Mahaprabhu's House

Ishan remained at Mahaprabhu's house to serve the family so was fortunate that he got the chances of serving Mahaprabhu, Nityananda, Gadadhar and other associates Vaishnavas.

Dukhi became Sukhi

One day there all started to bathe Mahaprabhu with pots after pots of water. One maid servant assisted the followers by bringing huge amount of water from the Ganga. To see much quantity of water supply Mahaprabhu knew the source that a little girl was bringing water fro the Ganga. Mahaprabhu asked the name of the girl.

She replied – Dukhi my name is' in low voice.

Mahaprabhu answered – No, it can't be your name as sorrow. You are serving for the Vaishnavas and you deserve the name of a happy girl. You must be happy. Let be your name Sukhi (Happy). Since all started to call her Sukhi. We may be sure that getting boon from Mahaprabhu the girl once became happy.

Narayani got blessings from Mahaprabhu Sri Gourangadev

Mahaprabhu Sri Gourangadev's love showered on many people of different trades, banana cone seller Sridhr, Suklambar Brahmachari and a little girl of four Narayani too. At Sri Baas Angan in Nabadwip when Mahaprabhu was engaged with chanting and dancing almost the whole day, one day He found a little girl of about four years' old crying for something. This little girl was Narayani, daughter of Sri Baas's deceased eldest brother Nalini. Her crying drew the attention of Lord Sri Gouranga.

Mahaprabhu told her- "why you are crying mum".

The girl yet remained silent for a while and then again started to cry.

Mahaprabhu then advised – "If you want to cry, cry for Lord Sri Krishna, utter Sri Krishna. He is the Lord of us. He can give everything if He desires. Cry for Him"

Surprisingly the four years' child started to cry by saying 'Haa Krishna, Krishna, Krishna Hey' and tears from her eyes started to fall.

To see it Mahaprabhu was pleased and blessed her. Mahaprabhu gave her the end of food eaten up almost every day while she was in Nabadwip.

Later Narayani was married to one Brahmin person of Kumarhatta named Baikunthadas. Unfortunately, that Baikuntha expired leaving her pregnant. Sri Baas brought this fatherless and husbandless carrying girl to his house at Kumarhatta. There on Krishnaa dwadashi (12th day of new moon) in 1429 Saka widow Narayani gave birth to a male baby. This baby afterwards became Vrindavandas, the Vyas of Sri Chaitanyalila. He wrote the Sri Chaitanya Bhagawat and still it gives the readers and devotees the maximum information of Nabadwiplila and others of Sri Chaitanyadev and His all associates.

Index